STATE V. JACKSON

Fifth Edition

STATE V. JACKSON

Fifth Edition

Laurence M. Rose
Professor Emeritus and
Director, Litigation Skills Program
University of Miami School of Law

Frank D. Rothschild
Attorney at Law
Kilauea, Hawaii

Hon. Rebecca Sitterly
Presiding Judge, Civil Division, Grand Jury Division (Ret.)
Albuquerque, New Mexico and
Grand Rapids, Michigan

Based on the original case file *Flinders v. Mismo*
created by Abraham P. Ordover

NATIONAL INSTITUTE FOR TRIAL ADVOCACY

Address inquiries to:
Reprint Permission
National Institute for Trial Advocacy
1685 38th Street, Suite 200
Boulder, CO 80301-2735
Phone: (800) 225-6482
Fax: (720) 890-7069
Email: permissions@nita.org

ISBN 978-1-60156-713-0
eISBN 978-1-60156-714-7
FBA 1713

ACKNOWLEDGMENTS

The authors would like to thank the following people for their assistance in the creation of this case file:

Abraham P. Ordover, Atlanta, Georgia, for his work in writing the original case file that provides the foundation for this updated version;

Hon. Tommy Jewell, former Second Judicial District Court, Presiding Juvenile Court Judge, Albuquerque, New Mexico, for his portrayal of the banker John Anderson;

Marjorie Martin, Esq., former Assistant District Attorney, Albuquerque, New Mexico, for her portrayal of Sonia Peterson;

Amy Diaz, Esq., Albuquerque, New Mexico, for her portrayal of Marie Williams;

Brad Hall, Esq., Albuquerque, New Mexico, for his portrayal of Arthur Jackson;

R. Thomas Dawe, Esq., Albuquerque, New Mexico, for his portrayal of the examining attorney in the depositions of Marie Williams and John Anderson;

Lieutenant William A. Dunn, Commercial Crimes Bureau, Sheriff Leroy D. Baca, and the men and women of the Los Angeles County Sheriff's Department for their generous provision of fire scene photographs and video clips of High Temperature Accelerant fires, all of which are used in this case file with the express written permission of the Los Angeles County Sheriff's Department;

Senior Criminalists Vickie Clawson and Phil T. Teramoto of the Los Angeles County Sheriff's Department Scientific Services Bureau for their assistance with the Accelerant Analysis Report;

and a very special thanks to Detective Ed Nordskog, Los Angeles County Sheriff's Department, Arson Explosives Unit and author of "Torched" Minds, a study of serial arsonists, for his invaluable assistance navigating the complexities of the National Fire Protection Agency Guideline 921 and for providing excellent film footage of fire scenes for use in this file

CONTENTS

CASE SUMMARY

This criminal action was originally brought by the State of Nita against Arthur Jackson and Sonia Peterson. It is claimed that the two arranged with George Avery to destroy the Flinders Aluminum Fabrication Corporation plant on November 16, YR-1, by burning the plant. Avery died in the fire. The two defendants were charged with commercial arson.

The case went to trial in YR-0 and resulted in a mistrial due to a hung jury, which voted nine to three to convict. Thereafter, Sonia Peterson pled guilty to conspiracy to commit a felony and agreed to testify against Arthur Jackson. The transcripts from the first trial are reproduced here.

SPECIAL INSTRUCTIONS

When this case file is used for a full bench or jury trial, the following witnesses may be called:

State:

Marie Williams *K*

John Anderson

Sonia Peterson — *direct exam*

Donald Olsen *K*

Open: Kaitlyn

Close: Mike

Voir dire Mike then Kaitlyn

Defense:

Janice Jackson *K*

David Pinkus *K*

Matthew Korn — *Cross*

Arthur Jackson (optional)

It has been stipulated that Exhibits 19 through 23 are business records as defined by section 803(6) and 803(8) of the Federal Rules of Evidence, and that witnesses could be called who would identify and testify accordingly. It has been stipulated that the video clips of the Flinders, Fass, and Yaphank fires (Exhibits 26 through 28) are actual footage of those fires.

It is agreed that a claim was filed by Flinders Aluminum under its insurance policy, the claim was denied by the Mismo Fire Insurance Company and that Flinders has filed a lawsuit seeking the proceeds of the policy. That case is pending.

All years in these materials are stated in the following form:

- YR-0 indicates the actual year in which the case is being tried (i.e., the present year);
- YR-1 indicates the next preceding year (please use the actual year);
- YR-2 indicates the second preceding year (please use the actual year), etc.

Electronic versions of the exhibits (in color), including videos and a PowerPoint slideshow, are available for download from NITA's Digital Download Center, here:

http://bit.ly/1P20Jea

Password: Jackson5

SUGGESTED TIME LIMITS FOR FULL TRIAL

Voir Dire   10 minutes per side (5 minutes per attorney when teamed up)

Opening Statement   20 minutes per side

Witness Examination   120 minutes per side

Closing Argument   20 minutes per side

IN THE CIRCUIT COURT OF
DARROW COUNTY, STATE OF NITA
CRIMINAL DIVISION

THE STATE OF NITA,

v.

CASE NO. CR-70410-1

ARTHUR JACKSON,
SONIA PETERSON,

Defendants.

INFORMATION

Sandra Harris, State Attorney of Darrow County, Nita, hereby charges the following offense under the Criminal Code of the State of Nita:

That on November 16, YR-1, at 187 River Road, Nita City, Nita, Arthur Jackson and Sonia Peterson committed the crime of Commercial Arson, a violation of Nita Revised Criminal Code Section 672.7, a felony, in that they personally or through an agent, did intentionally, willfully, and unlawfully damage by fire or explosion, a building or structure for the purpose of making a false insurance claim that would benefit Arthur Jackson and Sonia Peterson or an entity controlled by, or owned by, Arthur Jackson and/or Sonia Peterson.

Sandra Harris

Sandra Harris
Darrow County State Attorney
DATED: March 19, YR-0

REVISED CRIMINAL CODE

Section 672.7 Commercial Arson

1. A person commits the crime of commercial arson if the person personally or through an agent, intentionally and willfully damages by fire or explosion a building or structure for the purpose of making a false insurance claim that would benefit the person or an entity controlled by, or owned by, the person.

2. Commercial Arson is a felony punishable by confinement in prison for a minimum period of ten years and a maximum period of twenty-five years, a fine of up to $10,000, or both.

Section 842.4 Conspiracy to Commit a Felony

1. A person commits the crime of conspiracy to commit a felony if the person agrees with another person to act together to commit an offense that is punishable as a felony, and that either the person or the other commits an act that is pursuant to the plan to commit the felonious offense.

2. Conspiracy to commit a felony is a felony that is punishable by confinement in prison for a period up to ten years, or a fine of $5,000, or both.

TRANSCRIPT OF TESTIMONY OF MARIE C. WILLIAMS

September 14, YR-0

MARIE C. WILLIAMS, called to testify by the State and having been duly sworn, testified as follows:

My name is Marie C. Williams. I am thirty-five years old. I live at 2242 169th Avenue, Nita City. I am single with no dependents and live alone. I was employed as a bookkeeper and assistant to the president of the Flinders Aluminum Fabrication Corporation in Nita City.

Y-10 bookkeeper
Y-5 assistant

I was hired as bookkeeper on October 1, YR-10. About five years ago, I was also given the title of assistant to the president. I held both positions until August YR-1. Thereafter, I held only the bookkeeper post. On December 1, YR-1, I was discharged by Mr. Arthur Jackson, the president of the company. I had worked directly for Mr. Jackson since I joined the company. Mr. Jackson and I had a close personal relationship up until August of YR-1, when he hired Sonia Peterson as his personal aide. Thereafter, my personal relationship with Mr. Jackson terminated. *ended relationship with Sonia*

He and I had been lovers since YR-4. Mr. Jackson is married and has three children, but he told me that he was very unhappy and promised that he would leave his wife. *leave wife?*

16   Q: Ms. Williams, what did Mr. Jackson say to you about his marriage?

17   A: He said that he was very unhappy at home, and he promised me that he was going

18   to leave his wife. But he never left her, and finally I realized that he had lied to me

19   all along about leaving her.

20   Q: What was your reaction when you realized that?

21   A: I was really, really angry with him, and I finally broke off our relationship that fall

22   when he hired Sonia Peterson.

20-40 workers

The company employed from twenty-five to forty workers, depending upon the amount of business it had. The company was administered largely by Mr. Jackson and me until Ms. Peterson was hired. A separate sales staff was employed. They had little to do with the central administrative functions. We also employed several people in the shipping department.

YR-2 $500K in loss

In YR-2, the company had a disastrous year. Losses for the year totaled some $500,000. The year 2011 was even worse. Losses for the first nine months totaled an additional $500,000. Bank loans of $400,000 became due on November 28. In October YR-1, Mr. Jackson attempted to renegotiate the loans with the lender, First Trust Bank. I participated in those negotiations with Mr. Jackson and Mr. Anderson, vice-president of the bank. The negotiations failed. The loans went unpaid pending receipt of the fire insurance money.

At one meeting with Mr. Anderson, Mr. Jackson spoke of the Avery "designs" and the company's plans to get into the automobile market. Anderson seemed skeptical and requested drawings, market studies, and the like.

At no time were any such studies undertaken by the company. Nor do I recall any negotiations with any automobile manufacturer.

Mr. Anderson also requested that we supply the bank with current financial information. Mr. Jackson never asked me to prepare and send such data to the bank. I don't know if he, Ms. Peterson, or anyone else ever sent the information.

On July 14, YR-1, Mr. Jackson informed me that if the company didn't pick up new accounts in the last half of the year, it would go under. He complained bitterly of financial problems throughout the months that followed.

Sometime in early September, I overheard a conversation between Mr. Jackson and Ms. Peterson in which she offered to put him in touch with someone named Avery, who, she said, could solve his financial problems. I first saw them sitting and talking by looking through the door to Mr. Jackson's office that is across from my office. I then walked over to that doorway and, staying out of sight, heard their conversation. With regard to Mr. Avery, I also heard Ms. Peterson describe him as a "torch" to Mr. Jackson. As best I can recall, the exact words she used were something like: "I know a man named George Avery who can solve all of your financial problems. George is a real torch; he could light up this business for you."

On September 15, YR-1, Mr. Avery came to the plant and met with Mr. Jackson. Afterwards, Mr. Jackson asked me to draw a company check to George Avery for $10,000 and give him both the check and one of our spare plant keys. Mr. Jackson told me Mr. Avery was a tool and die designer who would soon be working at the plant to design dies for fabricating parts for use in automobiles. Exhibit 18 is the check I gave to Mr. Avery that day. As I recall, he started working at the plant on October 1.

Also in September, Mr. Jackson contacted the insurance company and increased the fire insurance coverage on the plant, effective October 1. I wrote the check for the increased premium.

I worked late on November 16. I recall that Mr. Jackson came back to the plant at 7:00 p.m. Avery had come in at about 6:30 p.m. One crew was finishing up a rush job. They left at about 6:45 p.m. I was surprised to hear machinery in operation after the last crew had left. I started to go downstairs to check out the matter when I met Mr. Jackson. He was surprised and annoyed to see me there and ordered me to leave at once. I did so. The plant burned down that evening. Avery died in the fire.

1   Q: When did you see Mr. Jackson next?

2   A: It was about a day or two after the fire.

3   Q: What did you say to each other?

4   A: I told him right off that I suspected that he had paid Avery to burn down

5   the building in order to get the insurance money.

6   Q: How did he respond?

7   A: He denied it. He said he didn't do it.

8   Q: What action did you take based upon your suspicions?

9   A: I didn't do or say anything right away, but about ten days later, Mr. Jackson fired me.

10   It was after that that I went to the police and talked to Detective O'Brien, and I told

11   him what I suspected Mr. Jackson had done.

It is true that I no longer care for Mr. Jackson, but that is not why I am willing to testify here. I am telling the truth.

Certified by:

Ann E. Hall

Ann E. Hall
Certified Shorthand Reporter (CSR)

TRANSCRIPT OF TESTIMONY OF JOHN ANDERSON

September 17, YR-0

JOHN ANDERSON, called to testify by the State and having been sworn, testified as follows:

My name is John Anderson. I am vice president of First Trust Bank in Nita City, and I am in charge of commercial lending for the bank. I graduated from the University of Kansas in YR-21 with a Business Administration degree. I then attended Northwestern University in Chicago and received a Master's in Business Administration in YR-17. I received the National Chamber of Commerce Fellowship Grant in my final year, and used it to complete a study of innovative ways to finance new business development in urban areas. My area of concentration while in school was studying the reasons for capital flight from urban centers and methods for revitalizing urban business communities.

I moved to Nita City in YR-16 after completion of my fellowship and became employed at First Trust Bank as a loan officer in the residential department. I was able to transfer to the commercial department in YR-15, as my primary interest is in commercial and business lending. I was a commercial loan officer from YR-15 to YR-7. At that time, the bank reorganized and established a Workout Division devoted solely to resolving lending difficulties with companies in default, or at risk of default, on their commercial loans. I was the manager of that division from its inception to YR-6, when I was promoted to the position of vice president in charge of all commercial lending, the position I still hold today. I have maintained a direct interest in the Workout Division, and I often still engage with customers and staff in coming up with creative solutions for troubled loans.

Flinders Aluminum Company had an outstanding loan which was in the amount of $400,000. Payment of this amount and accrued interest was due November 28, YR-1. The loan had been taken out five years earlier and was a balloon loan, with interest-only payments due on a quarterly basis. The interest payments had been kept current.

During the month of October of that year, I had several meetings with Mr. Arthur Jackson. On one occasion, he was accompanied by an aide, Ms. Marie Williams. I don't recall that Ms. Williams talked during the meeting. She did not bring any documents with her to the meeting.

During these meetings, Mr. Jackson sought to refinance the $400,000 loan. His company, he said, was not in a position to make the payment. It had suffered losses of approximately $1,000,000 in the two previous years. The Flinders loan was collateralized with inventory and equipment, but there was no other collateral or a personal guarantee. *Could have defaulted*

Mr. Jackson informed me of a plan to change Flinders' aluminum fabrication processes from siding used in the housing industry to automobile parts for General Motors or other vehicle manufacturers. He said he had employed a new tool and die designer for that purpose and gave me a copy of his resumé. He wanted to establish a long-term financing plan for Flinders to accomplish the transition to the new product line.

1   Q: What information did you ask for, Mr. Anderson?

2   A: I asked for the current financial data. That included the balance sheet, profit and loss

3   statements, pro forma statements, market analysis. I asked for tax returns.

4   Q: What information did you request concerning the designs?

5   A: I wanted to see a design of the product.

6   Q: What did Mr. Jackson say?

7   A: Mr. Jackson said that they were working on it, and that they would get it into the

8   bank shortly.

9   Q: What was the discussion about the possibility of additional collateral for the loan?

10   A: I didn't ask for additional collateral at that time.

I wrote the loan review committee to indicate that we might become an investor in the new venture if it went forward. The bank refused the renegotiation of the existing loan. No current financial information was made available to us by Mr. Jackson.

We took no action on the financing of the new product line. No concrete proposal was ever submitted to us. Nor did we receive the data that we requested.

Certified by:

Ann E. Hall

Ann E. Hall
Certified Shorthand Reporter (CSR)

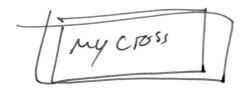

TRANSCRIPT OF TESTIMONY ARTHUR JACKSON

September 18, YR-0

ARTHUR JACKSON, called to testify by the Defense and having been duly sworn, testified as follows:

My name is Arthur Jackson. I just turned forty, and I am married. My wife, Janice, is thirty-eight years old, and we are currently separated. In the past few years, we have had some problems and *Dec-1* disagreements, but it all seemed to come to a head after the fire at the plant. In mid-December YR-1, we both agreed that it would be best if I moved out of the family home at 11 Purple Martin Lane, Nita City. I moved into an apartment at 1200 East Gate, Nita City, and I've been living there since. I am the president and sole stockholder of Flinders Aluminum Fabrication Corporation. I purchased the stock of the company in YR-12. Prior to my acquisition of Flinders, I was assistant to the president of Cosgrove Aluminum Company for three years. I am a graduate of Nita University and hold an MBA degree from Nita.

The Flinders Corporation was housed in a large, old building on the riverfront. The building, made mostly out of wood and brick, was located at 187 River Road in Nita City. The Flinders building had 50,000 square feet of space, spread out equally over four floors. The executive offices, including mine and my administrative assistant's, were in the front part of the building on the second floor. While in operation, the company employed between twenty-five and forty workers, depending on the amount of business we had. However, the company has no current operations because of the destruction of its plant.

On November 16, YR-1, the company suffered a disastrous fire. On January 3, YR-0, Fire Marshal Olsen questioned me and implied that I had started the fire or had Sonia Peterson and/or George Avery do so. They showed me a company check to Avery in the amount of $10,000. George Avery was a designer of tools and dies. I retained his services in September YR-1, to assist us in broadening our product line. We had been primarily in the business of fabricating aluminum windows and siding for the home construction market. That market had collapsed. The company had suffered great losses—about $1 million—in the past two years.

19	Q:	Mr. Jackson, how did you first hear about George Avery?
20	A:	George Avery was recommended to me by Sonia, Sonia Peterson, my administrative
21		assistant. She knew of his work from Yaphank, and spoke very highly of his designs.
22	Q:	Well, what did you do before hiring him?
23	A:	She discussed his qualifications with me, and then I interviewed him, and after
24		I interviewed him, I retained him.

Avery's office was located on the third floor. He had some splendid suggestions for selling aluminum parts to General Motors for use in place of steel in cars. We were studying that idea in November of YR-1.

The idea that Avery was an arsonist is absurd. He was a brilliant designer. His death in the fire was a terrible tragedy. The $10,000 payment to Avery was simply a basic retainer. If his program was successful, he was to receive an additional $100,000.

Fire Marshal Olsen suggested that Avery had burned the Yaphank plant and was implicated in another fire. I know nothing of these matters and find them impossible to believe.

I worked late the evening of November 16, but late hours were not unusual for me; nor, for that matter, were late hours unusual for George Avery.

10	Q:	Who did you talk to before you left that night?
11	A:	I talked with George Avery. It was about 6:45 p.m.
12	Q:	What did he say to you?
13	A:	He said that he was going to work a little longer.
14	Q:	Did you say anything back to him?
15	A:	No, I didn't. That was normal.
16	Q:	Did you see anybody else before you left that night?
17	A:	As a matter of fact, I did. I bumped into Marie Williams.
18	Q:	What time was that?
19	A:	That was closer to 7 o'clock.
20	Q:	What did you say to her?
21	A:	Well, she doesn't usually work late, and actually I thought she looked really tired.
22		And I said, "Marie, you look beat. You ought to go home."

Fire Marshal Olsen suggested that I needed money badly. I had no substantial personal needs, but the company did. At one point, I sent an email to my wife asking for a loan for the business. The company had lost quite a bit of money in the last couple of years. In October of YR-1, I told my wife that I needed a loan of at least $100,000. My wife refused to loan the money to me and told me to use my own assets. I told her that my own money was not enough to do the job. I have stocks valued at about $150,000, and my wife and I jointly own our home, which is valued at $350,000.

Also, my wife inherited some $350,000 from the estate of her father. That amount has been invested in common stocks of large corporations, including IBM, GM, and General Electric. As of the date of the fire, my wife and I were still living together.

Contrary to what the police suggested, I have no women friends. I did have an affair with Marie Williams, but that ended last fall. Marie Williams was my administrative aide for almost five years. However, in August of YR-1, I demoted her to her former position of bookkeeper.

In July YR-1, I got an email from Sonia Peterson expressing interest in working for Flinders, and I emailed her back the next day to set up an interview. I then hired her in early August as my new administrative aide. Ms. Peterson is thirty-three years old, and she performed her duties quite well. The police, undoubtedly echoing my wife, contended that I was having an affair with Ms. Peterson. This is not true. Ms. Williams was insanely jealous of Ms. Peterson. Her jealousy caused me to end our relationship. Her baseless charges of arson ultimately caused me to discharge her.

My business was really my whole life. Partly because of this, my wife and I quarreled heatedly over the past several months. She claimed I was having a relationship with Sonia Peterson. I denied this, but I knew my wife believed that I was lying. My wife also accused me of being intimate with Marie Williams. Both Marie and I denied that any such relationship existed. My wife and I separated on December 15, YR-1. Our separation was largely due to the Peterson business, but there were some financial considerations as well. My wife has custody of our three children: Phyllis, who is twelve; Harry, who is ten; and Ambrose, who is six. I should also note that my wife complained that she was the only one who always had to pay for any extras the family required.

Although Flinders had experienced problems, I felt certain that the business would improve this year. My retention of George Avery shows that I was optimistic at that time. His idea was sound. Auto manufacturers have, in fact, purchased millions of dollars of aluminum parts for replacement of heavier steel parts in their cars. I had every reason to believe this idea would turn the company around.

It would have required a major infusion of new capital into the business to retool. At the time, the company had a loan with First Trust Bank that we took out in November YR-6. We were required to pay back the entire principal in one balloon payment and had to pay accrued interest every quarter. We were able to keep up the interest payments. Payment on the principal in the amount of $400,000 plus accrued interest for that quarter was due November 28, YR-1. I personally guaranteed the loan, but there was no other collateral. There was no mortgage on the Flinders plant and land which was owned by the company, and the value of the land alone was worth more than the balance due on the loan.

In October YR-1, I met with John Anderson, vice president of the bank, on several occasions. I sought to refinance the $400,000 loan soon due and to begin consideration of major new financing for the retooling of the plant. Ms. Williams attended at least one of those meetings.

The bank refused to refinance the $400,000 loan, but was prepared to negotiate on the retooling matter once it saw Avery's ideas reduced to working designs. I gave Anderson a copy of Avery's resumé. Anderson also demanded that I submit current financials on the company together with market studies and projections covering the new product line.

1   Q: Mr. Jackson, what did you do to meet the bank's requests?

2   A: We were considering what to do at the time of the fire. I needed Avery's designs in

3   order to respond to those requests, and I was planning to contact General Motors

4   with those designs, and other manufacturers. But those designs were lost in the fire.

I was home when I received a phone call about 9:45 p.m. The police told me there was a fire at the plant and I rushed there only to see the building destroyed.

The authorities investigated the fire and concluded that it was of suspicious origin. They did not, however, arrest me or anyone else. I am aware that Chief Olsen contends that hydrochloric acid was used to start the fire. That material is regularly used in the fabrication process. We always kept five acid-resistant plastic drums on hand, each of which contained ten gallons of the acid. The acid was kept in a storage room on the first floor. No one "started" the fire. I do not know how it started.

The increase in Flinders' fire insurance effective October 1, YR-1, was simply a recognition of the effect of inflation. It was normal for me to increase the insurance coverage on the plant from time to time.

Certified by:

Ann E. Hall

Ann E. Hall
Certified Shorthand Reporter (CSR)

TRANSCRIPT OF TESTIMONY OF JANICE JACKSON

September 18, YR-0

JANICE JACKSON, called to testify on by the Defense and having been sworn, testified as follows:

I am Janice Jackson. I am thirty-eight years old. My address is 11 Purple Martin Lane, Nita City. I am separated from Arthur Jackson, who lives at 1200 East Gate. We have three children, Phyllis, twelve; Harry, ten; and Ambrose, six. We separated on December 15, YR-1.

I believe that Arthur had an affair with Sonia Peterson. It was not the first time he has had an affair. He had previously been involved with Marie Williams, but he broke off that relationship when I threatened to leave him. I cannot prove he had a relationship with Sonia Peterson, and he denies it. But I don't believe him. He has violated my trust and we just can't live together anymore. I believe we will get a divorce, but our uncertain financial situation has put that on hold. *Cantlet*

Yes, the financial situation before the fire was also precarious. You see, I have my own money, $350,000 which I inherited from my father. It is invested in large companies, such as General Motors, and IBM, and is now worth between $750,000 and $1 million. I won't touch it since I view it as my children's future. My husband has his own money and stock, and he solely owns his company. All of these items are separate. He gave me money each month to pay for the house, clothing, and groceries. I never really knew how much he made, or where his money was kept. He spent it all on the business, and probably his girlfriends.

The business was totally separate, and it was his whole life. He loved that business and the people who worked for him. To Arthur, it was a great challenge to stay ahead of the competition and build Flinders into a national firm. He spent more time there than at our house, or with me and the children. Yes, we fought over that too. He always said he was doing it to provide for us, but I told him that he needed to be with the family more. I always paid for vacations with the kids; he was never with us.

I believe that his affair with Marie Williams began in YR-4. She was the bookkeeper at the office. It got to a point that I confronted him in July YR-1, and threatened to leave him. He vowed to break it off and said it would never happen again. The only reason I stayed with him that long, and stay with him at all now, is for the children. I think that he may have stopped his affair with Marie when Sonia Peterson started at the company. He and Sonia were always "meeting" and talking on the phone. Although I can't prove he had an affair with Sonia, it really didn't matter. In fact we stopped sleeping in the same room (whenever he was home at all) in September YR-1.

In YR-1, around October 4 or 5, Arthur emailed me asking for a $100,000 loan. I emailed him that there was no way I was going to lend him any of my money. He told me that he was going to the company bank and that a bank loan was due soon, and he wanted to use some money to deal with the bank and help the business. I told him to use his own money, or get his girlfriend, Sonia, to help. Exhibit 30 is the email he sent me, and Exhibit 31 is my reply.

On November 16, YR-1, the night of the fire, Arthur came home at about 7:30 p.m. We had dinner with the children and then watched some television. Arthur told me that he was a little preoccupied that night, because his new design engineer was working late on the new product designs. He had talked about this project several times in the months before, and was really optimistic that his fortune, and our financial picture, would brighten up soon. He was planning to redirect the company into a completely new field and had hired some kind of design guru to help him make this shift. In fact, he said this new man was going to "save his butt." I knew the company had been having a tough time and was happy to see Arthur so enthused about turning things around. At about 9:45 p.m., the phone rang. I answered it. It was the police. They told me that there was a fire at the plant. I told Arthur. He was really shaken. He said that he was going there right away, and he left.

Arthur has not been the best husband or father, but he has never done anything to cause me to believe that he would burn down the business. I'm certain he did no such thing.

Certified by:

Ann E. Hall

Ann E. Hall
Certified Shorthand Reporter (CSR)

[My direct

TRANSCRIPT OF TESTIMONY OF SONIA PETERSON
September 19, YR-0

SONIA PETERSON, called to testify by the Defense and having been duly sworn, testified as follows:

I am Sonia Peterson. I live at 88 Charing Cross Muse, Nita City. I am thirty-three years old. I was employed by the Flinders Company from August YR-1, until mid-January YR-0. I served as an administrative aide to Mr. Jackson, the president of the company. I am presently unemployed, and my only income is my unemployment check, modest child support, and a small disability check for my son Brad. I have been looking for employment in the area of marketing and business and have had several interviews so far, but I have not been successful.

I am a single mother with two children, Mark (fourteen) and Brad (eight). Brad is autistic and needs at-home care which I am providing at present. I graduated from Nita State University in YR-12 with a bachelor's degree in marketing. Upon graduation, I worked at the Firehouse Insurance Company commercial department for four years. I then moved to the Yaphank Company, where I did marketing with strategic planning for six years when I was let go after a fire. At Yaphank, I oversaw the commercial and industrial storm shutter development.

Knows about resume

After Yaphank, I went in with a few partners to begin a consulting business and was the president of the firm. It was called Peterson, Miltown and Associates and was a venture capital solicitor for start-up companies. Although I wrote excellent business plans for the clients, my partners stole the clients and left me with substantial debts and no medical insurance benefits for my family. I did not sue my former partners, as I did not have funds for an attorney or the costs of litigation. In YR-2, I was able to obtain coverage under the Affordable Care Act for myself and my children, and I am struggling to pay the unsubsidized premium payments.

In July YR-1, I contacted Arthur Jackson, who I had heard was in financial trouble and looking for a turn-around strategy. Exhibit 32 is the initial email I sent him. He got back to me right away. Exhibit 34 is his reply. We set up a meeting the very next week. He told me that if we were successful, I was going to be a shareholder if the company went public. He also told me of some vague concepts about retooling the plant to produce new products, and it was clear that he needed to have a business plan and help for a marketing project. He was focused on changing to aluminum auto parts, which I did not have experience with, but I told him I would be able to develop a business plan no matter what the underlying product was. Jackson told me that he wanted to raise some capital to turn the business around, but that he didn't want to use the equity in the building and land to recapitalize due to some "community property" issues. He agreed to bring me on board right after our first meeting. I gave him my references from Yaphank, but I don't believe he checked them—at least he never told me he did. *What community - wife doesn't own anything*

When I arrived at Flinders, I helped draft a business plan, reorganize the files, do a marketing leaflet, and set up PowerPoint presentation packages. I was also told by Jackson to keep the plans from Marie. Williams and not discuss them with her, but I didn't really know why. I had the plan, leaflet, and PowerPoint presentations on my computer that was destroyed in the fire. Unfortunately, we did not have a "cloud" account or other backup program installed, although we had planned to sign up with Carbonite in December. The company did not yet have the funds to back up all of the computers used in the building.

I was familiar with the financial problems of the company. It had suffered substantial losses in YR-2 and YR-1. These losses amounted to almost $1,000,000. Moreover, the company owed $400,000 to First Trust Bank, due November 28, YR-1. Mr. Jackson was negotiating with Mr. Anderson of the bank to handle the $400,000 loan and the proposed retooling. Those negotiations were not proceeding well, according to Mr. Jackson, although I do not remember the specifics of what Mr. Jackson said about those meetings.

I understand that Anderson wanted projections and market studies done in connection with the retooling. We lacked the expertise to do such studies. I assumed we would hire an independent expert to prepare this data. We hadn't gotten that far when the fire put an end to the plans. I was never asked to, nor did I, send any information to the bank.

In September or October YR-1, I recommended George Avery, a tool and die designer, to Mr. Jackson. Avery had been hired by my former employer, the Yaphank Company, and I had heard he had done excellent design work for them. He also did work for Fass Meatpacking. The Yaphank plant did burn down shortly after Avery was hired, but certainly he had nothing to do with that. After all, Yaphank was rebuilt.

1	Q:	Ms. Peterson, what did you do to check on Avery's background?
2	A:	Well, I didn't check on his credentials, but I was familiar with his background. I knew
3		that he was an independent type. He liked to work as an independent contractor
4		and move around a lot. In addition to working as a tool and die designer for the
5		Yaphank Company and Fass Meatpacking, he also worked for General Dynamics
6		and McDonnell Douglas and American Motors Company.
7	Q:	What else did you know about his background?
8	A:	Well, I knew that he was a graduate engineer, and that he'd attended Cornell
9		and MIT.
10	Q:	How do you know that?
11	A:	Well, I never checked on his degrees, I didn't call the schools, but I do remember that

12		from his resumé.
13	Q:	Do you know whether Mr. Jackson checked?
14	A:	I do not know. I never talked to Mr. Jackson as to whether he checked on Mr. Avery's
15		credentials.

As I understand it, there are some wild assertions that I was having an affair with Mr. Jackson. Actually, I find him a good man, but unattractive.

I also have been told that Ms. Williams says I described Mr. Avery as a "torch." Ms. Williams is mistaken. I did not use the word "torch" at all or in any context. Although Ms. Williams says she was positioned outside Mr. Jackson's office when she supposedly overheard this conversation, she still did not hear the conversation correctly, as I did not make that statement. I simply felt that Mr. Avery was a talented tool and die person based upon having worked with him and having heard other people talk about him. Mr. Avery seemed like a nice and rather quiet person. At one point, I went to the company picnic with him at Yaphank—just as friends. We never dated, and we were never romantically involved.

Certified by:

Ann E. Hall

Ann E. Hall
Certified Shorthand Reporter (CSR)

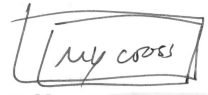
my cross

TRANSCRIPT OF TESTIMONY OF MATTHEW KORN

September 19, YR-0

MATTHEW KORN, called to testify by the Defense and having been duly sworn, testified as follows:

My name is Matthew Korn. I am president of Yaphank Company, which manufactures metal storm shutters.

In June YR-2, I became acquainted with George Avery, who applied to our company for a position as a tool and die designer. I interviewed him and he presented himself well. I was interested in his experience in connection with a new process I was thinking of developing; it was a crimping process to make our shutter edges more user friendly. I checked out Avery's references at McDonnell Douglas, General Dynamics, and Ross Metal. I know Jack Darnell, the division chief at General Dynamics, and I sent him an email asking about Avery in early June YR-2. Jack got back to me the same day saying Avery was a loner but his work was fine. Exhibit 35 is my email to Jack and his response to me. The other references also described Avery as a loner but very talented. I tried to check out his academic references at Cornell and MIT, which were listed on his resumé, but could not confirm them. The people I spoke with said that there was no record of his attendance under that name. But that didn't really matter to me, as his work references were excellent. *resume bullshit*

Shortly after Avery began his work, we suffered a disastrous fire in our plant. In fact we were closed for a period of time and laid off most of our employees, including Avery. I do know that Avery moved to the Fass plant to work and I used him for two to three months as a part-time consultant after we rebuilt the plant with the insurance proceeds.

Sonia Peterson worked for me from YR-8 to YR-2, but we had to let her go after the fire. She was a good marketing manager. I did not know her well, but only in connection with the business. I do know that she knew Avery while he was with us, as their offices were near each other and they came together to the office cookout in June.

I also am familiar with Chief Olsen. After our fire, he made lots of noise regarding the fire, claiming it was arson. Nothing ever came from his noise and I told him to either bring me up on charges or shut up. It was only after I threatened to sue him that he stopped talking about our fire.

It is true that our company was having certain financial problems before the fire and that we used hydrochloric acid in large amounts as part of our manufacturing process. I don't see what that's got to do with anything.

Certified by:

Ann E. Hall

Ann E. Hall
Certified Shorthand Reporter (CSR)

IN THE CIRCUIT COURT OF
DARROW COUNTY, STATE OF NITA
CRIMINAL DIVISION

THE STATE OF NITA,

v.   CASE NO. CR-70410-1

ARTHUR JACKSON,
SONIA PETERSON,

Defendants.

PLEA AGREEMENT

COMES NOW, Sandra Harris, State Attorney of Darrow County, Nita, by and through the under-signed Assistant State Attorney and hereby enters into this contract for a plea agreement with the defendant, Sonia Peterson.

The terms of the agreement are as follows:

1. The defendant shall plead guilty to one (1) count of conspiracy as charged in the amended information filed in this cause. The Court shall adjudicate the defendant guilty and sentence the defendant to three years of probation. The defendant's plea of guilty shall be irrevocable.

2. In addition to all of the standard conditions of probation, the following special conditions of probation are made part of the defendant's sentence and the defendant expressly agrees to these special conditions of probation.

   a. The defendant agrees to be debriefed by any local, state, or federal law enforcement agents at the direction of the State Attorney with regards to her knowledge of, or partici-pation in, any criminal activity occurring inside and outside of Nita City, Nita.

   b. The defendant agrees to give complete and truthful information in any such debriefings and specifically agrees not to falsely implicate any person.

   c. The defendant agrees to testify at any statements, depositions, or before any court or grand jury when called upon to do by the State Attorney, the court, or any other party with an interest in the litigation.

   d. The defendant agrees to act as a protected source in undercover investigations at the di-rection of the State Attorney.

3. The defendant must not claim any privilege or Fifth Amendment right to remain silent when questioned about the circumstances of the instant case or any other criminal acts of which she has knowledge.

Defendant's Initial *SP*

4. The parties agree that this agreement provides immunity from prosecution of the defendant for her direct or indirect involvement as a principal in the crime charged in the initial information.

5. The defendant agrees to submit to polygraph examinations at the direction of the State Attorney to determine the truthfulness of any statements or testimony provided pursuant to this Agreement and further agrees that the results of such examination shall be admissible against her in any probation violation hearing that may result. The State Attorney agrees that the defendant cannot be precluded from introducing evidence of compliance at any such hearing.

6. All of the agreements between the State of Nita and the defendant are contained within this plea agreement. There are no other agreements between the Office of the State Attorney and the defendant.

Wherefore, the State of Nita and the defendant do hereby move this Honorable Court to accept and ratify this Plea Agreement, after taking the appropriate plea colloquy and meeting all other requirements for the acceptance of a plea.

This agreement being entered into on the 10th day of December YR-0, in Nita City, Nita.

So agreed,

Darrow County State Attorney

Heather Hall

By:

Assistant State Attorney

Sonia Peterson

Sonia Peterson

Defendant

Ryan James

Attorney for Defendant

NOTES OF INTERVIEW: SONIA PETERSON

By State Attorney

December 10, YR-0

Ms. Peterson admitted that she and Jackson conspired to burn down the Flinders building. One night in early September YR-1, after a particularly late night working, Arthur grabbed her and kissed her. She really needed the job, so she really didn't protest. They ended up having sexual relations that night at the office. According to Peterson that was the only such occurrence in their relationship. Thereafter, she always made excuses to make sure that she would never be "available" if he made another pass. She is not happy to talk about that night's event, and she also knows that Jackson will deny the occurrence of that evening.

The night that she and Arthur were together, she made an offhand remark that they would work together to have Flinders rise from the ashes "like a phoenix." Arthur responded by saying he "would like to make the place ashes." The next day at the office, she told him that she knew a man named Avery whom she had dated and worked with at Yaphank, and who had told her that he had burned down the Yaphank and Fass plants for money using the on-hand hydrochloric acid as a means to start the fires. I asked if she had called Avery a "torch," and she told me that she may have used that word. Then she told him that she would introduce him to Avery. Arthur said to her, "Now that is strategic planning, and if it all works, there will be a bonus in it for you."

She introduced Avery to Jackson the next week in mid-September and urged Jackson to appear to be pursuing the possible bank financing with First Trust Bank. She suggested that these bank discussions would provide an alibi when the fire occurred. After the fire, she was to get half of Avery's "separation compensation" of $100,000.

On the night of the fire, Jackson and Avery told her to stay home with her children. After the fire, when she heard that Avery had died, she was afraid that she might be discovered due to her previous relationship with Avery. She talked with Jackson about Avery's death. Jackson told her to "keep your mouth shut and this will all go away." She admitted to lying during her testimony at the first trial and followed his directions, but when the verdict was hung she began to worry about her children, and that is why she asked her lawyer to make the deal to plead.

Exhibit 1

Mismo Fire Insurance Policy

THE MISMO FIRE INSURANCE COMPANY

FIRE INSURANCE POLICY

No. 951946

AGREEMENT between the Mismo Fire Insurance Company (hereinafter the "Company") and the Flinders Aluminum Fabrication Corporation (hereinafter the "Insured").

The policy is to take effect January 1, YR-10.

FACE AMOUNT: $835,000.

INSURED PREMISES: The plant and property of the insured located at 187 River Road, Nita City, Nita 99997

ENDORSEMENTS:

    Face amount: Increased to $1,125,000, January 1, YR-5.

    Face amount: Increased to $1,667,000, October 1, YR-1.

[The standard fire insurance policy is omitted. Clause 9 of that policy states as follows:]

9.   ARSON: The Company shall not be liable for loss caused by or resulting from arson where the same was occasioned by the deliberate acts of the insured or any agents thereof.

are the amts correct

Exhibit 2

Olsen Field Report

CITY OF NITA
BUREAU OF FIRE INVESTIGATION

FIELD REPORT

Inv. __Flinders Aluminum__   Date of Inv. <u>11/16 and 11/17/YR-1</u>

Time of Alarm __8:30 p.m.__   Date of Alarm <u>11/16/ YR-1</u>

Fire Location __187 River Road, Nita City__

Type of Building __Ind. Plant; wood, brick; circa YR-97__

Cause of Fire __Hydrochloric acid intentionally released and encountering an open flame.__

Fire Department __Nita__

Occupant __Flinders Aluminum__

       Address __same__

Owner __Arthur Jackson__

       Address __11 Purple Martin Lane, Nita City__

Arrests _____

Deaths __(1) male; cauc.__   Closed_____ Open <u>XX</u>

Arson Detective __Olsen__   Police at Scene: Yes <u>XX</u> No ___

Preliminary Classification <u>Incendiary</u>

Remarks: HCL stored in large quantities on the premises was used to cause the explosion and fire. The localized destruction and eyewitness accounts of the rapid horizontal spread of the fire support this classification. Obtained video footage of fire from local news channel. Photographs of deceased taken after fire extinguished. This investigator at scene beginning 6:00 a.m. 11/17. Photographs of scene and location of deceased obtained 11/17. Suggest file remain open for further investigation.

Date: __11/17/YR-1__   *Donald Olsen*

                                       Investigator: Donald Olsen, Chief

Exhibit 3

Olsen Report of Supplemental Investigation

CITY OF NITA

BUREAU OF FIRE INVESTIGATION

REPORT OF SUPPLEMENTAL INVESTIGATION

Re: Flinders Aluminum Fabrication Corp., 187 River Rd, Nita City

Reference: Field Report, BRI 202, 11/17/YR-1

The deceased found on the premises has been identified as one George Avery, age fifty-seven, of 2318 Crescent Street, Nita City.

Cause of death, as established by medical examiner, was from multiple injuries sustained in the explosion.

Avery has been investigated previously by this office in connection with fires at the Yaphank Co. and Fass Meatpacking Co.

This investigator conducted both investigations at the time of the fires, and I have reviewed the videotape footage of the Yaphank fire and the Fass fire, which I had obtained from a local news channel and stored in the archives of our offices. The video footage of the Flinders fire compared to the video footage of the Yaphank and Fass fires indicates similarities in flame color, smoke color, and flame reaction to water. Avery had been employed by Yaphank as a designer of metal fittings. The fire occurred two weeks after his initial employment. Although the Yaphank fire was likely arson, there was insufficient evidence upon which to base an arrest.

The Yaphank plant was rebuilt following the fire. Avery was re-employed by them on a part-time basis for several months.

The Fass fire was also likely caused by arson. Mr. Avery was a paid consultant to Fass. He was retained by them six weeks prior to the fire. The Fass fire was caused by the explosion of HC1, apparently ignited by a mixture of calcium hypochlorite with a common hair shampoo. Oxidation within minutes caused a hot fire which likely ignited the HC1. The company went out of business following the fire.

This could have been the setup at Flinders. The traces of the igniter in this case were likely washed away by the fire hoses. However, it appears that one of the machines in the shop had been operating just prior to the fire. HC1 combining with hot metal can create an explosive situation.

Donald Olsen

Date: 11/27/YR-1   Investigator: Donald Olsen, Chief

Form BFI 204

Exhibit 4

Olsen Bureau Report

CITY OF NITA
BUREAU OF FIRE INVESTIGATION

REPORT

TO: Detective O'Brien, Nita City Police Department

FROM: Chief Fire Marshal Olsen

                 Bureau of Fire Investigation

DATE: December 18, YR-1

SUBJECT: Report of fire occurring on the night of November 16, YR-1, at an industrial plant located at 187 River Road, Nita City, owned by Flinders Aluminum Corporation.

BUILDING DESCRIPTION:

The fire occurred at an industrial plant. The building was four stories high, constructed of wood and brick, approximately 50,000 square feet overall and built in YR-93. The building contained an inventory of aluminum products.

DESCRIPTION OF FIRE:

The fire occurred on November 16, YR-1, at approximately 8:00 p.m. The fire was discovered by Alison Smith, who was passing by the plant on the way home from visiting a friend. Ms. Smith contacted the Nita City Fire Department at 8:30 p.m. Four units responded to the fire and arrived at the scene at 8:36 p.m.

The fire was of considerable size at the time the first firetrucks arrived at the scene. The smoke was reddish brown and was accompanied by large flames. The fire was large and spreading in a horizontal direction at a rapid speed. It took five hours, an unusually long time, to bring the fire under control. The flames became brighter and changed color when hit with a stream of water from a hose. An inspection of the debris indicated that there was one independent origin of the fire.

DAMAGE:

The building was almost entirely destroyed. Only one section of the northwest wall of the building was left standing. The fire caused one fatality. This individual was identified as George Avery, a white male, approximately fifty-seven years old.

ADDITIONAL FINDINGS:

A chemical analysis of the ashes revealed the presence of hydrochloric acid (HCl). An examination of the remaining structure showed that the windows either had been open or were blown out.

My investigation was conducted per the NFPA 921 Guide for Fire and Explosion Investigations. I ruled out the usual accidental causes. Accidental fires involve those for which the proven cause does not involve an intentional human act to ignite or spread the fire. The point of origin was a large combination storeroom and machine shop on the first floor of the building. Analysis of the debris, burn patterns, and damage indicated a "hot spot" in that location and that an explosion had taken place.

I have inspected these premises many times in the course of fire prevention duties. No faulty electrical wiring or motors were found. No heating devices were located near the point of origin. Machines used in coating the aluminum were in the area and apparently had been in use up until shortly before the fire. These machines were equipped with timer starting devices and were capable of being preset to operate automatically.

Hydrochloric acid is not flammable in and of itself. However, under certain conditions it is highly explosive. These conditions would have to have been intentionally created for ignition of the instant fire.

The proper storage of hydrochloric acid is imperative. Many materials provide unsuitable containers because hydrochloric acid is so highly corrosive. The choice of container is dependent upon the quantity of acid to be stored. When a large quantity of hydrochloric acid (such as 10,000 gallons) is to be stored, then the proper container would be a plastic or rubber-lined steel tank. This combination would have the structural strength of steel and the nonreactive nature of rubber or plastic. When a smaller quantity of hydrochloric acid (such as fifty gallons) is stored, a plastic drum is recommended. Because hydrochloric acid may contain traces of hydrofluoric acid, which attacks fiberglass, as a safety measure a container of fiberglass lined with plastic is not recommended.

When a plastic container or liner is used for storage, the hydrochloric acid cannot compromise the integrity of the plastic and leak out of the container. This is because plastic is chemically inert to the acid. Glass could also be used, but problems arise with the tendency for glass to break and the difficulty of repair. An acid leak would occur if the container was ruptured (by a forklift, for instance), if the container was faulty, if the container was sabotaged, or if the wrong drum was used.

Serious problems may arise if hydrochloric acid is improperly stored and leaks out of its container. If the acid contacts a ferrous metal, such as steel, then hydrogen is generated. Hydrogen is an explosive gas. The chemical formula of this reaction is:

$$2HCl + Fe \qquad FeCl_2 + H_2$$
$$(L) \quad (S) \qquad (S) \quad (G)$$

(L) = liquid; (S) = solid; (G) = gas

Whereas hydrochloric acid is not in itself explosive, if it contacts steel it will release hydrogen. If the hydrogen encounters an ignition source, an explosion would occur.

CAUSE OF FIRE:

The reddish brown color of the smoke, together with the large flames, indicates that substances containing nitrocellulose fiber, sulfur, or sulfuric, nitric, or hydrochloric acid were burning. The fact that flames burned brighter and changed color when hit with water is another indication that an accelerant was used. Difficulty in extinguishing the fire also points to the use of an accelerant. A chemical analysis of the ashes showed that hydrochloric acid, an explosive substance when combined with hot metal, in fact was burning. When HCl comes in contact with ferrous metals, hydrogen is released, and when hydrogen is combined with air, it may cause an explosive situation. Although hydrochloric acid is normally present in the plant, scarring of the concrete floor plus chemical analysis showed that an unusually large amount was located at the point of origin of the fire. Moreover, the magnitude of the fire and its rapid spreading indicate that several hundred gallons of the acid likely were splashed about the source of the fire. Normally, a plant of this type and size would maintain a supply of approximately fifty gallons of hydrochloric acid for cleaning purposes. This would likely be stored in one place. Analysis of the debris indicates an explosion at the point of origin, likely caused by a time release igniter, possibly the preset timer of one of the machines or calcium hypochlorite mixed with shampoo.

The large flames are an indication that the fire was well ventilated. Favorable ventilation conditions were created by the explosion in order to ensure that the ensuing fire spread quickly. Such unusually good ventilation would not normally be present since the building is enclosed and the windows would be shut on a November evening. Lack of ventilation would be necessary for the explosion. That, in turn, would create the ventilation needed for the fire to spread. A professional would know how to blow out the windows. Another factor pointing to deliberate ignition is the rapid progress made by the fire. According to Ms. Smith from 8:30 p.m., when she first discovered the fire, to 8:36 p.m., when the first fire trucks arrived at the scene, the fire had spread tremendously.

Field Investigator Henderson, who was present at the scene of the blaze, reported that the flames spread quickly in a horizontal direction. This is another indication that good ventilation existed. Fire sweeps upward until it is blocked by some obstruction. When the fire is blocked, it travels through any available crack or opening. If there are no openings, the flames spread horizontally until the fire can sweep around the obstruction. When good ventilation conditions do not exist, the horizontal spread is slow. The fact that the horizontal travel of the fire was rapid indicates that favorable ventilation existed.

George Avery, whose body was found in the debris of the machine shop, died of multiple injuries resulting from the explosions. The autopsy report indicates that the fatal injury was to the chest. Field Investigator Henderson also obtained photographs of Avery's body at the scene, as well as photographs of the location of the body marked by outline tape the following morning. FI Henderson also took a photograph of the plant debris and remaining wall section after the fire was extinguished.

We had previously come into contact with Avery in connection with other investigations. Our normal practice in an arson case is to investigate all persons connected with the enterprise and, without exception, an investigation of any corpse found on the premises would be made.

Our investigation of Avery showed that he had been linked to two other fires that were of incendiary origin. One fire destroyed a factory owned by the Yaphank Co. Mr. Avery had been employed by Yaphank for only two weeks prior to the fire. The other fire destroyed a warehouse at the Fass Meatpacking Co. Although these fires were likely the result of arson, there was insufficient evidence for an arrest. Mr. Avery, who was associated with these businesses when the fires occurred, was questioned on both occasions. This marshal conducted both investigations. In connection with this investigation, I reviewed Avery's resumé which I obtained from John Anderson at First Trust Bank. I checked with Cornell and MIT, schools Avery indicated on his resumé he had graduated from. Neither had any record of George Avery.

Contrary to popular belief, a substantial number of arsonists are trapped and killed in their own fires. For the most part, these persons are less than skilled at the techniques of arson. It is less likely that a professional arsonist would be caught in his own fire, but not particularly unusual.

CONCLUSION:

This marshal concludes that the fire was the result of arson. This conclusion is based upon the following factors:

1. The unusually large amount of hydrochloric acid that was located at the point of origin of the fire and apparently splashed about the room. Hydrogen likely was released and, in combination with ferrous metal, exploded by some sort of time release device that malfunctioned.

2. The unusually rapid spread of the fire, caused by favorable ventilation conditions not normally present.

3. The presence of George Avery in the building at the time of the fire.

Submitted by:

Donald Olsen

Donald Olsen
Chief Fire Marshal

Exhibit 5

Memorandum

TO: File

FROM: Chief Olsen

DATE: January 3, YR-0

RE: Flinders Company Fire, 11/16/YR-1

I interviewed Arthur Jackson, president of Flinders Aluminum Fabrication Corp., at his home on January 3, YR-0. Jackson denied the arson. He admitted that Peterson had introduced him to Avery, the alleged designer. He seemed surprised (he said) by my assertion that Avery was a torch. I told him of Avery's work at the Yaphank Co. and that the Yaphank plant had burned down. He identified Avery as the man he hired to do design work, but denied knowledge of any fire at Yaphank. He reacted the same way when I told him of Avery's connection with the Fass Co., which also suffered a terrible fire.

He admitted paying Avery $10,000.

He admitted that HCl was kept at the plant in quantities of about fifty gallons.

I asked him if he personally checked on Avery's credentials listed on his résumé or any references Avery may have supplied. He said he left such matters to Ms. Peterson.

He said he had no motive because his wife had assets of around $300,000 and he had personal assets of about $150,000.

On the evening of the fire, he visited the plant to pick up some papers from his office. This was at about 7 p.m. He left the plant by 7:30 p.m.

He said he dismissed Marie Williams from her position because she was becoming a pest and an embarrassment. He admitted that they had been lovers and asked if this information could be kept confidential.

Exhibit 6

Olsen Resumé

RESUMÉ OF DONALD OLSEN

BIOGRAPHICAL:

Born in Nita City, Nita in YR-52. Married to Rita Olsen, two children.

EDUCATIONAL BACKGROUND:

Graduated from Darrow High School in Nita City in YR-43. Attended classes at Lincoln Community College in general curriculum from YR-34 to YR-32. Enlisted in United States Army in YR-32 and served in Fort Sill, Oklahoma and Weisenstadt, Germany APO until YR-27.

Attended Nita Fire Department Training School in East Meadow, Nita in YR-26, including basic courses in fire investigation and firefighting.

Completed an additional six-month arson investigation course at Nita Fire Department Training School, and received certification by state and national training review agencies.

WORK HISTORY:

YR-25 to YR-20	Fireman, East Meadow Fire Department, East Meadow, Nita; arson investigator for two years.
YR-20 to YR-10	Marshal, Arson Bureau, East Meadow Fire Department, Nita
YR-10 to YR-5	Chief, Arson Bureau, East Meadow Fire Department, Nita
YR-5 to present	Chief, Nita Fire Department Bureau of Fire Investigation

Exhibit 7

Flinders Floor Plan (First floor)

Exhibit 8

Flinders Floor Plan (Second floor)

Exhibit 9

Flinders Floor Plan (Third floor)

Exhibit 10

Flinders Floor Plan (Fourth floor)

Flinders Plant

Fourth Floor Plan

Exhibit 11

Photograph of Flinders Pre-Fire

Exhibit 12

Photograph of Flinders Post-Fire

Exhibit 13

Photograph of Fass Meatpacking Co.

Exhibit 14

Photograph of Yaphank Co.

Exhibit 15

George Avery Resumé

2318 Crescent Street, Nita City
Phone (620) 980-6845
Email avery@nitamail.nita

George A. Avery

Education	YR-39 to YR-35	Cornell University, Bachelor of Science in Engineering Graduated *cum laude*
	YR-35	Science Prize from University Board of Trustees
	YR-35 to YR-33	Massachusetts Institute of Technology, Masters of Arts Industrial Engineering Master's Thesis: "Metallurgical Processes in Industrial Grade Steel Fastener Failures"
Professional experience	YR-33 to YR-30	Crown Engineering, Intern, Draftsman
	YR-30 to YR-29	Crown Engineering, Journeyman Draftsman
	YR-28 to YR-26	Ross Metal Industries, Senior Draftsman
	YR-26 to YR-23	Ross Metal Industries, Design Protocol
	YR-22 to YR-21	American Motors, Senior Draftsman
	YR-20 to YR-19	BMI, Senior Draftsman
	YR-18 to YR-17	General Dynamics, Senior Draftsman
	YR-16 to YR-15	McDonnell Douglas, Engine Tool and Die Unit
	YR-15 to YR-13	McDonnell Douglas, Design Protocol Division
	YR-12 to YR-11	Ford Motor Company Parts Integration
	YR-10 to YR-9	General Dynamics, Engine Parts Testing and Design
	YR-8 to YR-7	Ford Motor Company. Parts Integration
	YR-6 to YR-5	Macauley Equipment Manufacturing, Tool and Die Design
	YR-4 to YR-3	Jefferson Aeronautics, Inc. Tool and Die Design
	YR-2	Yaphank Company, Metal Fittings Design
	YR-1	Fass Meatpacking Company, Tool and Die Design Consultant
Patents and publications	YR-16	Patent Application for Manifest Coupler U.S. Patent No. A78-3847659328
References		Suzanne Barker, American Motors, (760) 474-7285 Henry Arnett, Ross Metal Industries, (630) 243-0956 Jack Darnell, General Dynamics Corporation, (890) 583-3487

Exhibit 16

George Avery Photograph

Exhibit 17

Photograph of Avery Body Outline

Exhibit 18

Avery Check

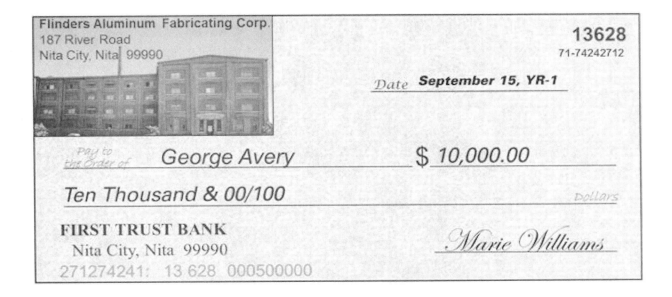

Flinders Aluminum Fabricating Corp.
187 River Road
Nita City, Nita 99990

13628
71-74242712

Date **September 15, YR-1**

Pay to
the Order of   George Avery $ 10,000.00

Ten Thousand & 00/100   Dollars

FIRST TRUST BANK
Nita City, Nita 99990   *Marie Williams*

271274241: 13 628 000500000

Exhibit 19

Autopsy Report

STATE OF NITA
COUNTY OF DARROW

Office of Medical Examiner

(721) 555-3200

County/City Building

Nita City, Nita 99990

AUTOPSY REPORT
George Avery

Information available at time of autopsy:

This fifty-seven-year-old Caucasian male was found beneath the debris of an explosion at a local aluminum plant.

Under the provisions of Nita Code 21-205, a postmortem examination including autopsy of the body is performed in the Darrow County Medical Examiner's Office on November 17, YR-1, commencing at 10:00 a.m.

External examination of the body:

The decedent is brought to the morgue in a disaster bag. Clothing includes a blue plaid, long-sleeve shirt on which the sleeves are burned and the seams on the sleeves are torn, a pair of blue jeans that have numerous types of particulate debris on them, a pair of white briefs, a pair of white crew socks, and a pair of white Nike tennis shoes. These items of clothing are forwarded to the Crime Laboratory.

This is the unembalmed body of a white male which weighs 175 pounds and measures six feet in height. The stature is mesomorphic, rigor mortis is generalized, and lividity is dorsal and not fixed and has a pinkish discoloration. No other decompositional changes are noted, and the overall appearance of the body is that of a well-developed white male, consistent with the stated age of fifty-seven years. The hair is light brown, of medium length, and shows frontal parietal balding. Portions of the hair in the frontal region have been scorched. The external auditory meati are unremarkable. The irises are blue and the pupils are equally dilated. The nasal and oral cavities contain a small amount of bloody froth. The teeth are the decedent's natural teeth and are in average condition. There are first-and second-degree burns over the skin of the face and cheeks and there is a 3.5 cm angulated laceration over the ramus of the right mandible, which is a full thickness laceration and appears to represent some impact with an object which has a right angle on its surface.

The neck is unremarkable.

The upper extremities are remarkable in that there are first- and second-degree burns over the skin of the hands and distal forearms, and there is a compound fracture of the right humerus.

The torso is remarkable in that there are numerous fractures of the ribs bilaterally that can be palpated through the skin. There are three small ecchymoses over the left pectoral region and there are numerous superficial scrapes over the skin of the lumbar region. On the back there is a three-inch in diameter circular contusion that is definitely patterned and is essentially a series of 1 cm arcs that form a "broken circle." It is located over the right scapula.

The external genitalia are those of a normal adult male, the penis is circumcised, and both testes are descended.

The lower extremities are remarkable only in that there are several ecchymoses over the anterior surfaces of both tibias that are of various ages, and there are several acute contusions over the right patella.

Internal examination of the body:

Head

The skin of the scalp is retracted in the usual manner, and there are several areas of soft tissue hemorrhage in the scalp over the right and left frontal parietal regions.

The underlying calvarium is intact, and upon its removal there is no blood in the epidural, subdural, or subarachnoid space. The cerebral gyri are moderately broadened and flattened, and the sulci are moderately obliterated. Coronal sectioning of the 1250 gram brain demonstrates no gross abnormalities other than cerebral edema. There is no herniation. The dura is reflected from the base of the skull, and there is no evidence of basilar skull trauma.

Chest and Abdomen

The skin of the chest and abdomen is opened with the usual Y-shaped incision, which demonstrates a 1 cm layer of yellow subcutaneous adipose tissue. There is moderate amount of hemorrhage in the subcutaneous fat over the chest and abdomen. Upon reflection of the skin flaps, the right ribs two through six can be palpated to be fractured in the axillary line, and the left ribs two through seven have been fractured in the anterior axillary line.

Upon removal of the chest plate, there is a bilateral hemothorax totaling two liters. The rib fractures have penetrated the parietal pleura and have caused bilateral pulmonary contusions and lacerations. Both lungs are collapsed.

The skin of the neck is dissected up to the angle of the jaw and there is no evidence of soft tissue trauma to the major airways or vital surrounding structure of the lateral neck compartments.

The thoracic and abdominal organs are examined in situ, then removed by the Virchow technique for serial examination.

Major Airways

The larynx, trachea, and major bronchi are unremarkable except that there is a small amount of blood adherent to the mucosa, and there is a moderate amount of soot in the airways.

Lungs

The right lung weighs 500 grams, and the left lung 460 grams. Both lungs are collapsed and atelectatic. There are bilateral pulmonary contusions, and there is mild anthracotic change on the pleural surfaces. There are no mass lesions seen on serial sectioning of the lungs. There are focal areas of parenchymal hemorrhage surrounding the pulmonary contusions, and the pulmonary veins have been lacerated bilaterally at the hila.

Heart

The heart weighs 290 grams. There is concentric left ventricle hypertrophy. The epicardium, endocardium, valve leaflets, and chordae tendineae are unremarkable. The coronary arteries show mild atherosclerotic plaquing, but the degree of occlusion is not significant.

Gastrointestinal Tract

The esophagus is unremarkable. The stomach contains two cups of partially digested food, which consists primarily of noodles with a small amount of slightly chewed meat which appears to be beef. The small bowel, large bowel, appendix, and rectum are unremarkable.

Hepatobiliary System

The liver weighs 1900 grams and is congested. The gall bladder contains 15 ml of watery green bile and no stones. The extra hepatic biliary ducts are patent.

Spleen

The spleen weighs 120 grams, has a wrinkled capsule, and has a small laceration near the posterior pole of the hilum. There are about 150 ml of blood in the splenic bed.

Pancreas

The pancreas weighs 110 grams, has a coarsely lobulated appearance and soft consistency on cross section.

Urinary System

The right kidney weighs 140 grams, and the left kidney 150 grams. Both capsules strip easily from the cortical surfaces, and the kidneys have the typical cortex and dark medulla consistent with "shock kidney." The ureters are unremarkable, and the bladder mucosa is within normal limits. The bladder contains about 150 ml of dilute urine.

Endocrines

The thyroid and adrenals are unremarkable. The parathyroids are not identified.

Great Vessels

The great vessels of the thorax and abdomen and the tributaries thereof are unremarkable except for acute trauma to the pulmonary veins noted above.

Other procedures:

1.   Blood and urine are submitted for toxicology.

2.   Documentary photographs are taken.

3.   Clothing is submitted to the Crime Laboratory for accelerant analysis.

4.   Autopsy diagrams marked with location of injuries.

Gross diagnoses:

1.   First- and second-degree burns to face and distal forearms and hands.

2.   Bilateral rib fractures and bilateral pneumothorax and hemothorax.

3.   Bilateral pulmonary contusions with lacerations of pulmonary vein.

4.   Fracture of right humerus.

5.   Laceration of spleen.

6.   Patterned contusion, back.

7.   Patterned laceration, skin over right mandible.

Causes of death:

BLUNT TRAUMA, PRIMARILY TO CHEST causing victim to hemorrhage into chest cavity. Combination of trauma from blow and blood in chest cavity resulted in collapse of lungs and inability to breathe.

Ronald Harrison

Ronald Harrison, MD
Medical Examiner
RH:sd

Date: November 18, YR-1

Exhibit 20

Autopsy Diagram (front-rear)

Exhibit 21

Autopsy Diagram (hand)

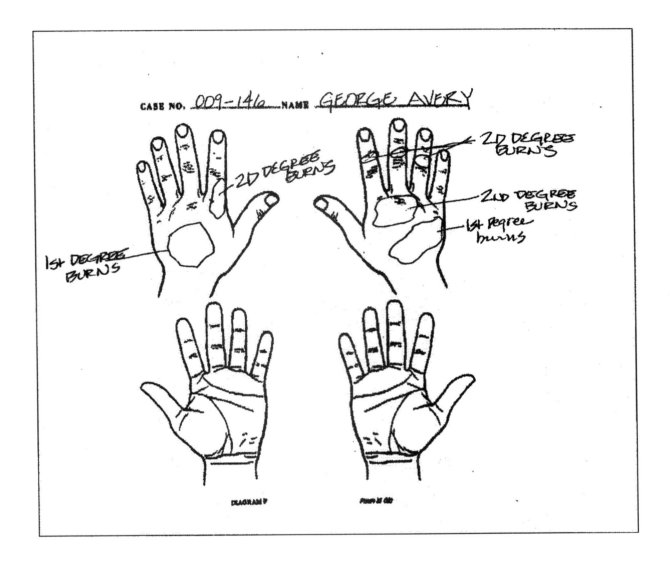

Exhibit 22

Autopsy Diagram (side)

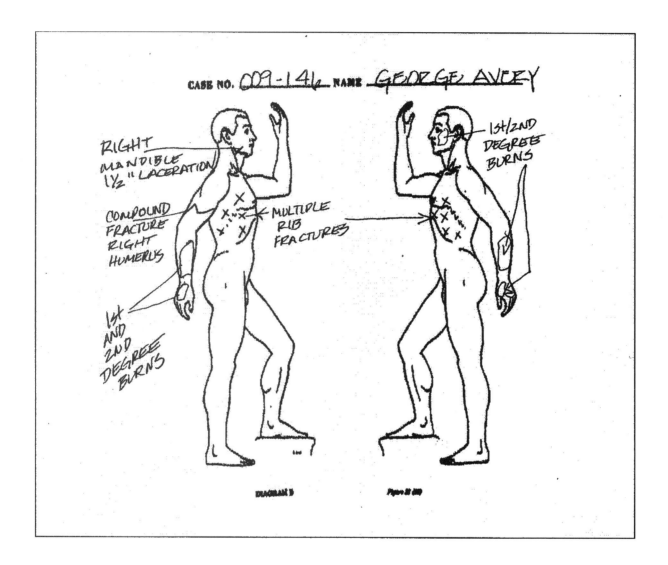

Exhibit 23

Accelerant Analysis Report

CITY OF NITA POLICE DEPARTMENT

CRIME LABORATORY

ACCELERANT ANALYSIS REPORT

Physical Evidence Section	Agency:	Bureau of Fire
232 Barnett	File:	6374
Nita City, Nita	Investigator:	Olsen
	Charge:	NC 20-305
Subject: Flinders Aluminum Fabrication Corp.	Report Date:	December 1, YR-1
	Examination by:	Victoria Faris, Senior Criminalist

At the request of Chief Fire Marshal Olsen, clothing samples were examined for the presence of hydrochloric acid, iron filings, and shampoo. The clothing samples were reportedly from the deceased, George Avery, and were forwarded to the Crime Laboratory by the Office of the Medical Examiner on November 17, YR-1. Returned to Olsen on December 1, YR-1.

Laboratory Examination

The following items were received:

Item 1, a blue plaid shirt with burnt sleeves

Item 2, blue jeans

Item 3, white briefs

Item 4, white crew socks

Item 5, a pair of white Nike athletic shoes

The clothing items were visually examined for particles, for stains indicative of acid exposure, and for shampoo residue. Stains on the blue jeans were tested for acidity (pH) and examined with X-ray fluorescence spectrometry (XRF) and chemical spot tests. Particulate debris from the blue jeans was examined with X-ray fluorescence spectrometry (XRF). A solid residue from the plaid shirt collar was tested for surfactant (sudsing) properties. Aqueous extracts of the soles of the Nike shoes were tested for pH and examined with X-ray fluorescence spectrometry (XRF) and chemical spot tests. The lower parts of the sleeves of the shirt were burnt away and could not be examined for pH.

Examination Conclusions and Observations

No indications of hydrochloric acid, such as acidity or chloride, were found on the blue jeans or the soles of the Nike shoes. This does not mean the items were not exposed to hydrochloric acid under circumstances in which it did not survive on the clothing, such as dilution or exposure to heat. A variety of metallic particles were found on the blue jeans, including aluminum, iron, and some with a composition of iron, nickel, and chromium, which are found in stainless steel. The solid residue from the left shirt collar exhibited sudsing properties when mixed with water, as would be expected from shampoo or soap products. No other tests were performed on the solid residue. This laboratory cannot determine the brand of shampoo.

Exhibit 24

Report of David Pinkus

RE: Fire at Flinders Aluminum Fabrication Corporation's industrial plant, 187 River Road, Nita City

DATE OF FIRE: November 16, YR-1   **DATE OF REPORT:** May 1, YR-0

I have thoroughly reviewed the report of Chief Fire Marshal Olsen. My analysis of the facts in his report leads me to conclude that the fire must be technically listed as an accident. My review and analysis are conducted pursuant to pertinent provisions of the National Fire Protection Association Guide 921. In the course of my analysis, I reviewed all reports and memos from Chief Olsen, the three fire videos of the fires at Fass, Yaphank, and Flinders, the autopsy report performed on George Avery, photographs of the scene taken close to the time of the Flinders fire, and the accelerant analysis report provided by the Crime Laboratory.

Hydrochloric acid is normally present at the plant because it is used to clean the aluminum products. Since it is stored in one place, this would explain the large quantity of hydrochloric acid at the point or origin of the fire. Chief Olsen's conclusion that hundreds of gallons were splashed about the room is pure conjecture based not on physical evidence, but upon the size of the fire. The explosion itself could explain the searing of the concrete and the presence of HCl in the debris. Given the elapsed time between ignition and observation, no conclusion as to the amount of acid involved or whether it was spread about is possible.

The smoke and flame of the fire were not observed until the fire was burning for one-half hour. By this time, the building was being consumed by the fire. At this point, the color of the smoke and flame is affected by the burning building and not the acid.

In my opinion, the rapid spread of the fire could have been caused by several factors. First, from my previous visits to the plant during fire prevention duties, the rooms were large, with considerable fuel loading, open, and provided favorable ventilation conditions that would encourage the fire to spread. Although the remaining structure showed that a window was open, there is no way of knowing if the other windows were open or closed, because most of the structure was destroyed. Second, since the building was very old, it was not constructed to prevent fire travel, nor was it constructed to prevent many causes of accidental fires. Third, an accidental explosion involving fifty gallons of hydrochloric acid would result in the conflagration described in Chief Olsen's report. Fourth, accidental explosion would account for the fatality. It is unlikely that a professional arsonist would be so careless as to be caught in a fire of his own making.

Chief Olsen has not ruled out, nor could he, the possibility that a leak in a storage drum holding HCl could have resulted in the introduction of the acid throughout the storage room. If the acid came into contact with hot ferrous metal from any cause, an explosion could result.

The sheer magnitude of the physical destruction caused by the explosion, fire, and the volume of water poured on the fire would have washed away evidence of accidental causes such as faulty wiring, cigarette butts, and the like.

In arson investigation, no finding of arson should be made until all possible accidental causes are ruled out. Since accidental causes of the fire have not been satisfactorily eliminated, I am unable to conclude that the fire was the result of arson. As to the presence of Mr. Avery, I agree with Chief Olsen that his background should be gone into in some detail. Some of that background is disquieting. However, there is insufficient evidence to establish that Avery is an arsonist. Moreover, there is little evidence in this case, other than circumstances, to link him to the fire.

Submitted by:

David Pinkus
David Pinkus

Exhibit 25

Pinkus Curriculum Vitae

DAVID G. PINKUS
CURRICULUM VITAE

YR-33–YR-29   *United States Navy*
Officer Candidate School
Service, Manila, Philippines; Guam

While in service, assigned various combat and non-combat duties. Received specialized training in fighting on-ship fires, including aircraft carriers, destroyers, and patrols. Was assigned supervisory responsibility for on-board firefighting teams during wartime operations. Achieved rank of lieutenant.

YR-28–YR-10   *Firefighter, Fire Investigator, Nita City Fire Department*

Attended Fireman Training Academy, Nita City, followed by two years' service as a firefighter for the Fire Department. Involved in multiple firefighting operations, including residential and commercial structures and involving multiple mechanisms of fire initiation.

Joined the National Fire Emergency Rescue team and engaged in forest fire fighting operations in Yellowstone National Park, Colorado, and Idaho.

Accepted for intensive training in arson investigation offered by Colorado College, followed by two years' service as an arson investigator in the Nita City Bureau of Fire Investigation.

YR-10–YR-5   *Deputy Fire Marshal, Nita City Bureau of Fire Investigation*

Appointed Deputy Fire Marshal in charge of arson investigation, and supervised an investigation team that grew from three investigators to twenty investigators.. Attended a series of six national seminars on aspects of arson investigation, including uses of accelerants, explosives, household compounds, and commonly available chemicals and ignition devices.

Have taught courses in arson investigation and investigative procedures at the Nita City Bureau of Fire Investigation and at the Nita Fire Department Training School in East Meadow.

Retired from the Bureau with commendation, February 6, YR-5.

YR-5 to Present   ***Consultant and Lecturer in Arson Investigation Techniques***

For past six years, have worked as a forensic consultant in both civil and criminal cases involving unexplained fires and explosions. Have worked for both plaintiffs and defendants in civil cases and both the state and the defendant in criminal cases. Have lectured at a number of seminars on the subject of modernizing arson investigation techniques.

PROFESSIONAL ASSOCIATIONS AND ORGANIZATIONS

Past president, Nita State Association of Firefighters
National Board Member, National Association of Firefighters
Member, Joint Task Force Nita City/County Arson Investigation Modernization
Member and Past Vice-President, National Emergency Response Team

PUBLICATIONS

National Association of Firefighters Newsletter, "Short Fuse Ignition Devices in Intentionally Set Fires," Vol. 4: 28–32 (YR-12)

Chapter, "Modern Techniques for Site Recovery of Accelerant Residue," in *Arson Investigation*, Houghton Miflin (YR-5)

Exhibit 26

Video of Flinders Fire (available via NITA's Digital Download Center)

http://bit.ly/1P20Jea

Password: Jackson5

Exhibit 27

Video of Yaphank Fire (available via NITA's Digital Download Center)

http://bit.ly/1P20Jea

Password: Jackson5

Exhibit 28

Video of Fass Fire (available via NITA's Digital Download Center)

http://bit.ly/1P20Jea

Password: Jackson5

Exhibit 29

Anderson Bank Memo

First Trust Bank
Nita City, Nita 12305

MEMORANDUM

TO: Gerald Laughlin
            Loan Review Committee

FROM: John Anderson, Vice President

DATE: October 15, YR-1

RE: Flinders Transition Plan

I have had several meetings this month with Arthur Jackson, President of Flinders Aluminum, in which he has requested new financing and an adjustment of current financing with the bank. I have reviewed the proposed concept of transitioning the Flinders Aluminum plant that currently manufactures siding for housing to an auto parts manufacturing plant and am seeking additional information from our client in this regard. Given the admitted recent earnings track record at Flinders, the time has come for such a transition and, if handled deftly, this could be a very promising investment. I have asked the client to provide financial data, market studies, tax returns, and product designs (surprisingly, none have been provided to date), which, if they pan out, will encourage our participation. The land value alone in this riverfront area could provide the requisite security for any investment.

I will advise when the follow-up information arrives.

Exhibit 30

Email to Janice Jackson from Arthur Jackson

Arthur Jackson

From: Arthur Jackson <arthur@flindersalum.nita>

Sent: Wednesday, October 5, YR-1 9:23 a.m.

To: Janice Jackson (jj@nitalink.nita)

Subject: A favor

Hi Janice:

I am really sorry that you and I are not talking.

As you know, business at the plant has been very slow since last year and we are having a hard time making ends meet. On top of that, we have a large loan with our bank that is due next month and I'm not sure we have enough cash on hand to make the payment. I have come up with a business plan that I believe will bring the company back, but in the meantime I need additional resources to bring this plan to fruition and work out my finances with the bank, so I'm hoping that you can loan me $100,000 out of your inheritance investments to tide me over until I turn things around.

Many thanks in advance,
Art

Arthur Jackson
President
Flinders Aluminum Fabrication Corporation
187 River Road
Nita City, Nita 99992
(952) 225-5000
arthur@flindersalum.nita

Exhibit 31

Email to Arthur Jackson from Janice Jackson

Janice Jackson

From: Janice Jackson <jj@nitalink.nita>

Sent: Thursday, October 6, YR-1 10:45 a.m.

To: Art Jackson

Subject: Not a chance!

I can't believe you think I would take money out of the account I am keeping for our children and their future to help you try to pull off some cockamamie plan to rescue your failing business. Use your own damn money or, absent that, ask your new girlfriend, Sonia, for the money.

Janice Jackson
1200 East Gate
Nita City, Nita 99993
jj@nitalink.nita

Arthur Jackson

From: Arthur Jackson <arthur@flindersalum.nita>

Sent: Wednesday, October 5, YR-1 9:23 a.m.

To: Janice Jackson (jj@nitalink.nita)

Subject: A favor

Hi Janice:

I am really sorry that you and I are not talking.

As you know, business at the plant has been very slow since last year and we are having a hard time making ends meet. On top of that, we have a large loan with our bank that is due next month and I'm not sure we have enough cash on hand to make the payment. I have come up with a business plan that I believe will bring the company back, but in the meantime I need additional resources to bring this plan to fruition and work out my finances with the bank, so I'm hoping that you can loan me $100,000 out of your inheritance investments to tide me over until I turn things around.

Many thanks in advance,
Art

Arthur Jackson
President
Flinders Aluminum Fabrication Corporation
187 River Road
Nita City, Nita 99992
(952) 225-5000
arthur@flindersalum.nita

Exhibit 32

Email to Arthur Jackson from Sonia Peterson

Sonia Peterson

From: Sonia Peterson <sonia@nitamail.nita>
Sent: Wednesday, July 10, YR-1 2:13 p.m.
To: Arthur Jackson (arthur@flindersalum.nita)
Subject: Introduction

Dear Mr. Jackson:

I believe we should meet. I have an extensive background in strategic planning, marketing, product development, and obtaining venture capital for startups and businesses in need of capital infusion. Word on the street is that Flinders is going through hard times and needs a turn-around strategy, which is right up my alley. And the timing couldn't be better, since I'm looking for a new challenge where I can get in on the ground floor of a solid, industrially based company.

My resumé is attached for your review. If you are interested, please call me at 952-639-0828 to set up an appointment.

Sonia Peterson
88 Charing Cross Muse
Nita City, Nita 99994
(952) 639-0828
sonia@nitamail.nita

Exhibit 33

Resumé of Sonia Peterson

SONIA PETERSON
88 CHARING CROSS MUSE
NITA CITY, NITA
952-639-0828
SONIA@NITAMAIL.NITA

Career Profile

Experienced Administrative Assistant with excellent organizational skills and emphasis on developing new businesses and product lines.

Skills and Proficiencies

- All standard word processing programs, including Word, Excel, and accounting and presentation software

- Marketing research and pro forma statements for business development and new product lines

- Customer service programming

- Business planning on monthly, quarterly, and annual basis

- Financial and credit research and presentations

- Employee benefit programs and human resource organization

- Purchasing and invoicing

Employment History

June YR-12–May YR-8   **Firehouse Insurance Company**

Entry-level position in commercial department. Responsible for transcription, customer contacts, correspondence, document review, and proofing. Was promoted after six months to assistant administrative supervisor of secretarial pool. After two years was promoted to administrative supervisor of the secretarial pool, with responsibilities for interfacing with management and establishing employee workforce and development planning.

June YR-8–June YR-2   **Yaphank Company**

Administrative supervisor of development of new product lines including commercial and industrial storm shutters and accompanying business plans for submission to lenders and potential customers. Responsible for market research, market development, customer contacts, and strategic long-term planning. Oversaw product line development from market entry stage to significant expansion of market share in sales of commercial and industrial shutters and window protection systems.

July YR-2–present   Peterson, Miltown & Associates

Partner in venture capital enterprise concentrating on start-up companies in the field of manufacturing. Client list includes several companies that have established success in manufacturing a variety of products, including automobile parts, brick veneer construction systems, commercial security devices, and cold weather paint application systems.

Education

YR-12   Nita State University

BA in Business, emphasis on marketing and development of new businesses. Graduated *magna cum laude*. Received Chamber of Commerce Award for "Ideas in Business Innovation," Spring Semester YR-12.

Exhibit 34

Email to Sonia Peterson from Arthur Jackson

Arthur Jackson

From: Arthur Jackson <arthur@flindersalum.nita>
Sent: Thursday, July 11, YR-1 8:15 a.m.
To: Sonia Peterson (sonia@nitamail.nita)
Subject: Introduction

Thank you, Ms. Peterson, for your interest in my company. You have an interesting background. I'm particularly impressed with your work at Yaphank and would like to hear more about it. Would you have time to meet with me at the plant sometime early next week?

Arthur
Arthur Jackson
President
Flinders Aluminum Fabrication Corporation
187 River Road
Nita City, Nita 99992
(952) 225-5000
arthur@flindersalum.nita

Sonia Peterson

From: Sonia Peterson <sonia@nitamail.nita>
Sent: Wednesday, July 10, YR-1 2:13 p.m.
To: Arthur Jackson (arthur@flindersalum.nita)
Subject: Introduction

Dear Mr. Jackson:
I believe we should meet. I have an extensive background in strategic planning, marketing, product development, and obtaining venture capital for startups and businesses in need of capital infusion. Word on the street is that Flinders is going through hard times and needs a turn-around strategy, which is right up my alley. And the timing couldn't be better, since I'm looking for a new challenge where I can get in on the ground floor of a solid, industrially based company.

My resumé is attached for your review. If you are interested, please call me at 952-639-0828 to set up an appointment.

Sonia Peterson
88 Charing Cross Muse
Nita City, Nita 99994
(952) 639-0828
sonia@nitamail.nita

Exhibit 35

Emails between Matthew Korn and Jack Darnell

Korn, Matthew

From: Jack Darnell [jack.darnell@generaldynamics.nita]
Sent: June 10, YR-2 1:18 p.m.
To: Korn, Matthew [mkorn@yaphankco.nita]
Subject: George A. Avery

Matt: To tell you the truth, I do not remember him well. He worked alone and did not socialize either during work or after with anyone. He was only there in my division for a short while, maybe three or four months before he left. His work for us was fine. I wish I had more info.

See you July 4 at the Club?

Jack

Jack Darnell
Division Chief
General Dynamics Corporation
1256 Alamo Parkway
East Meadow, Nita

From: Korn, Matthew [mkorn@yaphankco.nita]
Sent: June 10, YR-2 11:09 a.m.
To: Jack Darnell [jack.darnell@generaldynamics.nita]
Subject: George A. Avery

Jack: I hope this email finds you well. I am checking out George A. Avery, an engineer who I am thinking of hiring to assist with a tool and die design position. He has listed you as a reference and shows his employment at General Dynamics as a Senior Draftsman in YR-18 to YR-17 and working in Engine Parts Testing and Design in YR-10 to YR-9. What can you tell me about him?

Matt

Matthew Korn
President
Yaphank Company
1551 Green Street
Nita City, Nita

Exhibit 36

Pinkus Memorandum

MEMORANDUM

TO: Counsel for Mismo Fire Insurance

FROM: Legal Assistant

RE: David Pinkus

At your request, I have checked with several attorneys about defendant's fire expert in the Jackson case, David Pinkus.

Mr. Pinkus is known more by criminal attorneys for his opinions in alleged arson cases. He is thought of as fair minded and balanced in his approach. Both the prosecution and defense have retained him in such cases, as stated in his resumé. In the civil arena, Mr. Pinkus has been retained primarily (somewhere in the neighborhood of 90 percent of the time, from what I can tell) by members of the plaintiff's bar to refute charges of arson leveled by insurance companies when denying damage claims due to fire. Nobody I talked to remembers him ever testifying in civil court that a fire was purposefully set. Rather, he usually attacks the findings of the investigation team.

Based on counsel's 26(a)(2)(B) disclosure, he is paid $300 an hour for consulting work and report writing, $3,000 a day (and $2,000 for half a day) when testifying at deposition or in court, and has thus far billed $3,000 in this case for phone calls, meetings, review of material, and writing his report.

Exhibit 37

Excerpt from NFPA Guide 921*

Chapter 4 Basic Methodology

4.1 Nature of Fire Investigations. A fire or explosion investigation, is a complex endeavor involving skill, technology, knowledge, and science. The compilation of factual data, as well as an analysis of those facts, should be accomplished objectively, truthfully, and without expectation bias, preconception, or prejudice. The basic methodology of the fire investigation should rely on the use of a systematic approach and attention to all relevant details. The use of a systematic approach often will uncover new factual data for analysis, which may require previous conclusions to be reevaluated. With few exceptions, the proper methodology for a fire or explosion investigation is to first determine and establish the origin(s), then investigate the cause: circumstances, conditions, or agencies that brought the ignition source, fuel, and oxidant together.

4.2 Systematic Approach. The systematic approach recommended is that of the scientific method, which is used in the physical sciences. (*see Figure 4.3*).

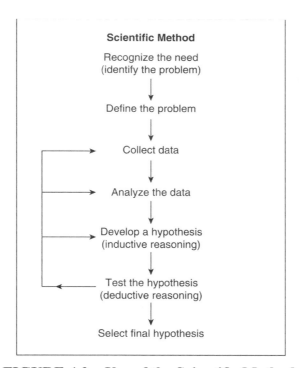

FIGURE 4.3   Use of the Scientific Method.

4.3.2 Define the Problem. Having determined that a problem exists, the investigator or analyst should define the manner in which the problem can be solved. In this case, a proper origin and cause investigation should be conducted. This is done by an examination of the scene and by a combination of other data collection methods, such as the review of previously conducted investigations of the incident, the interviewing of witnesses or other knowledgeable persons, and the results of scientific testing.

4.3.3 Collect Data. Facts about the fire incident are now collected by observation, experiment, or other direct data gathering means. The data collected is called empirical data because it is based on observation or experience and is capable of being verified or known to be true.

4.3.4 Analyze the Data. The scientific method requires that all data collected be analyzed. This is an essential step that must take place before the formation of the final hypothesis. The identification, gathering, and cataloging of data does not equate to data analysis. Analysis of the data is based on the knowledge, training, experience, and expertise of the individual doing the analysis. If the investigator lacks expertise to properly attribute meaning to a piece of data, then assistance should be sought. Understanding the meaning of the data will enable the investigator to form hypotheses based on the evidence, rather than on speculation.

4.3.5 Develop a Hypothesis (Inductive Reasoning). Based on the data analysis, the investigator produces a hypothesis, or hypotheses, to explain the phenomena, whether it be the nature of fire patterns, fire spread, identification of the origin, the ignition sequence, the fire cause, or the causes of damage or responsibility for the fire or explosion incident. This process is referred to as inductive reasoning. These hypotheses should be based solely on the empirical data that the investigator has collected through observation and then developed into explanations for the event, which are based upon the investigator's knowledge, training, experience, and expertise.

4.3.6 Test the Hypothesis (Deductive Reasoning). The investigator does not have a valid hypothesis unless it can stand the test of careful and serious challenge. Testing of the hypothesis is done by the principle of deductive reasoning, in which the investigator compares his or her hypothesis to all the known facts as well as the body of scientific knowledge associated with the phenomena relevant to the specific incident. A hypothesis can be tested either physically by conducting experiments or analytically by applying scientific principles in "thought experiments." When relying on experiments or research of others, the investigator must ensure that the conditions and circumstances are sufficiently similar. When the investigator relies on previously conducted research, references to the research relied upon should be noted. If the hypothesis cannot be supported, it should be discarded and alternate hypotheses should be developed and tested. This may include the collection of new data or the reanalysis of existing data. The testing process needs to be continued until all feasible hypotheses have been tested and one is determined to be uniquely consistent with the facts, and with the principles of science. If no hypothesis can withstand an examination by deductive reasoning, the issue should be considered undetermined.

4.3.6.1 Any hypothesis that is incapable of being tested is an invalid hypothesis. A hypothesis developed based on the absence of data is an example of a hypothesis that is incapable of being tested. The inability to refute a hypothesis does not mean that the hypothesis is true.

4.3.7 Avoid Presumption. Until data have been collected, no specific hypothesis can be reasonably formed or tested. All investigations of fire and explosion incidents should be approached by the investigator without presumption as to origin, ignition sequence, cause, fire spread, or responsibility for the incident until the use of scientific method has yielded testable hypotheses, which cannot be disproved by rigorous testing.

4.3.8 Expectation Bias. Expectation bias is a well-established phenomenon that occurs in scientific analysis when investigator(s) reach a premature conclusion without having examined or considered all of the relevant data. Instead of collecting and examining all of the data in a logical and unbiased manner to reach a scientifically reliable conclusion, the investigator(s) uses the premature determination to dictate investigative processes, analyses, and, ultimately, conclusions, in a way that is not scientifically valid. The introduction of expectation bias into the investigation results in the use of only that data that supports this previously formed conclusion and often results in the misinterpretation and/or the discarding of data that does not support the original opinion. Investigators are strongly cautioned to avoid expectation bias through proper use of the scientific method.

4.3.9 Confirmation Bias. Different hypotheses may be compatible with the same data. When using the scientific method, testing of hypotheses should be designed to disprove the hypothesis. Confirmation bias occurs when the investigator instead tries to prove the hypothesis. This can result in failure to consider alternate hypotheses. A hypothesis can be said to be valid only when rigorous testing has failed to disprove the hypothesis.

4.4.3 Conducting the Investigation. 4.4.3.1 It is during this stage of the investigation that an examination of the incident fire or explosion scene is conducted. The fundamental purpose of conducting an examination of any incident scene is to collect all of the available data and document the incident scene. The investigator should conduct an examination of the scene if it is available and collect data necessary to the analysis.

4.4.3.2 The actual investigation may include different steps and procedures, which will be determined by the purpose of the assignment. These steps and procedures are described in detail elsewhere in the document. A fire or explosion investigation may include all or some of the following tasks: a scene inspection or review of previous scene documentation done by others; scene documentation through photography and diagramming; evidence recognition, documentation, and preservation; witness interviews; review and analysis of the investigations of others; and identification and collection of data from other appropriate sources.

4.4.5 Analyzing the Incident. All collected and available data should be analyzed using the principles of the scientific method. Depending on the nature and scope of one's assignment, hypotheses should be developed and tested explaining the origin, ignition sequence, fire spread, fire cause or causes of damage or casualties, or responsibility for the incident.

4.4.6 Conclusions. Conclusions, which are final hypotheses, are drawn as a result of testing the hypotheses. Conclusions should be drawn according to the principles expressed in this guide and reported appropriately.

4.5 Level of Certainty. The level of certainty describes how strongly someone holds an opinion (conclusion). Someone may hold any opinion to a higher or lower level of certainty. That level is determined by assessing the investigator's confidence in the data, in the analysis of that data, and testing of hypotheses formed. That level of certainty may determine the practical application of the opinion, especially in legal proceedings.

18.6.5.1 Cause Undetermined. In the circumstance where all hypothesized fire causes have been eliminated and the investigator is left with no hypothesis that is evidenced by the facts of the investigation, the only choice for the investigator is to opine that the fire cause, or specific causal factors, remains undetermined. It is improper to base hypotheses on the absence of any supportive evidence (see 11.5.2, Types of Evidence). That is, it is improper to opine a specific ignition source that has no evidence to support it even though all other hypothesized sources were eliminated.

18.6.5 Inappropriate Use of the Process of Elimination. The process of determining the ignition source for a fire, by eliminating all ignition sources found, known, or believed to have been present in the area of origin, and then claiming such methodology is proof of an ignition source for which there is no evidence of its existence, is referred to by some investigators as "negative corpus." Negative corpus has typically been used in classifying fires as incendiary, although the process has also been used to characterize fires classified as accidental. This process is not consistent with the Scientific Method, is inappropriate, and should not be used because it generates un-testable hypotheses, and may result in incorrect determinations of the ignition source and first fuel ignited. Any hypothesis formulated for the causal factors (e.g., first fuel, ignition source, and ignition sequence), must be based on facts. Those facts are derived from evidence, observations, calculations, experiments, and the laws of science. Speculative information cannot be included in the analysis.

18.7.2 Inconsistent Data. It is unusual for all data items to be totally consistent with the selected hypothesis. Each piece of data should be analyzed for its reliability and value. Not all data in an analysis has the same value. Frequently, some analysis or witness statement will provide data that appears to be inconsistent. Contradictory data should be recognized and resolved. Incomplete data may make this difficult or impossible. If resolution is not possible, then the cause hypothesis should be re-evaluated.

18.7.4 Undetermined Fire Cause. The final opinion is only as good as the quality of the data used in reaching that opinion. If the level of certainty of the opinion is only "possible" or "suspected," the fire cause is unresolved and should be classified as "undetermined." This decision as to the level of certainty in data collected in the investigation or of any hypothesis drawn from an analysis of the data rests with the investigator.

19.2.1.1 Accidental Fire Cause. Accidental fires involve all those for which the proven cause does not involve an intentional human act to ignite or spread fire into an area where the fire should not be. When the intent of the person's action cannot be determined or proven to an acceptable level of certainty, the correct classification is undetermined. (See Section 18.6.)

19.2.1.3 Incendiary Fire Cause. The incendiary fire is one intentionally ignited under circumstances in which the person igniting the fire knows the fire should not be ignited. When the intent of the person's action cannot be determined or proven to an acceptable level of certainty, the correct classification is undetermined. (See Section 18.6.)

JURY INSTRUCTIONS

Preliminary Instruction 1 – Introduction

You have been selected as jurors and have taken an oath to well and truly try this cause. This trial will last one day. During the progress of the trial, there will be periods of time when the Court recesses. During those periods of time, you must not talk about this case among yourselves or with anyone else.

During the trial, do not talk to any of the parties, their lawyers, or any of the witnesses. If any attempt is made by anyone to talk to you concerning the matters here under consideration, you should immediately report that fact to the Court.

You should keep an open mind. You should not form or express an opinion during the trial and should reach no conclusion in this case until you have heard all of the evidence, the arguments of counsel, and the final instructions as to the law that will be given to you by the Court.

Preliminary Instruction 2 – Conduct of the Trial

First, the attorneys will have an opportunity to make opening statements. These statements are not evidence and should be considered only as a preview of what the attorneys expect the evidence will be.

Following the opening statements, witnesses will be called to testify. They will be placed under oath and questioned by the attorneys. Documents and other tangible exhibits may also be received as evidence. If an exhibit is given to you to examine, you should examine it carefully, individually, and without any comment.

It is counsel's right and duty to object when testimony or other evidence is being offered that he or she believes is not admissible. When the Court sustains an objection to a question, the jurors must disregard the question and the answer, if one has been given, and draw no inference from the question or answer or speculate as to what the witness would have said if permitted to answer. Jurors must also disregard evidence stricken from the record.

When the Court sustains an objection to any evidence, the jurors must disregard that evidence. When the Court overrules an objection to any evidence, the jurors must not give that evidence any more weight than if the objection had not been made.

When the evidence is completed, the attorneys will make final statements. These final statements are not evidence but are given to assist you in evaluating the evidence. The attorneys are also permitted to argue in an attempt to persuade you to a particular verdict. You may accept or reject those arguments as you see fit.

Finally, just before you retire to consider your verdict, I will give you further instructions on the law that applies to this case.

Final Instructions

Members of the jury, the evidence in this case has been completed, and I will now instruct you as to the law.

The law applicable to this case is stated in these instructions and it is your duty to follow all of them. You must not single out certain instructions and disregard others.

It is your duty to determine the facts, and to determine them only from the evidence in this case. You are to apply the law to the facts and in this way decide the case. You must not be governed or influenced by sympathy or prejudice for or against any party in this case. Your verdict must be based on evidence and not upon speculation, guess, or conjecture.

From time to time, the court has ruled on the admissibility of evidence. You must not concern yourselves with the reasons for these rulings. You should disregard questions and exhibits that were withdrawn or to which objections were sustained.

You should also disregard testimony and exhibits that the court has refused or stricken.

The evidence that you should consider consists only of the witnesses' testimonies and the exhibits the court has received.

Any evidence that was received for a limited purpose should not be considered by you for any other purpose.

You should consider all the evidence in the light of your own observations and experiences in life.

Neither by these instructions nor by any ruling or remark that I have made do I mean to indicate any opinion as to the facts or as to what your verdict should be.

1. Opening statements are made by the attorneys to acquaint you with the facts they expect to prove. Closing arguments are made by the attorneys to discuss the facts and circumstances in the case, and should be confined to the evidence and to reasonable inferences to be drawn therefrom. Neither opening statements nor closing arguments are evidence, and any statement or argument made by the attorneys that is not based on the evidence should be disregarded.

2. You are the sole judges of the credibility of the witnesses and of the weight to be given to the testimony of each witness. In determining what credit is to be given any witness, you may take into account his or her ability and opportunity to observe; his or her manner and appearance while testifying; any interest, bias, or prejudice he or she may have; the reasonableness of the testimony considered in the light of all the evidence; and any other factors that bear on the believability and weight of the witness's testimony.

3. You have heard evidence in this case from witnesses who testified as experts. The law allows experts to express an opinion on subjects involving their special knowledge, training and skill, experience, or research. While their opinions are allowed to be given, it is entirely within the province of the jury to determine what weight shall be given their testimony. Jurors are not bound by the testimony of experts; their testimony is to be weighed as that of any other witness.

4. The law recognizes two kinds of evidence: direct and circumstantial. Direct evidence proves a fact directly; that is, the evidence by itself, if true, establishes the fact. Circumstantial evidence is the proof of facts or circumstances that give rise to a reasonable inference of other facts; that is, circumstantial evidence proves a fact indirectly in that it follows from other facts or circumstances according to common experience and observations in life. An eyewitness is a common example of direct evidence, while human footprints are circumstantial evidence that a person was present.

   The law makes no distinction between direct and circumstantial evidence as to the degree or amount of proof required, and each should be considered according to whatever weight or value it may have. All of the evidence should be considered and evaluated by you in arriving at your verdict.

5. The information in this case is the formal method of accusing the defendant of a crime and placing him on trial. It is not any evidence against the defendant and does not create any inference of guilt. The State has the burden of proving beyond a reasonable doubt every essential element of the crime charged in the information or any of the crimes included therein.

6. The State has the burden of proving the guilt of the defendant beyond a reasonable doubt, and this burden remains on the State throughout the case. The defendant is not required to prove his innocence.

7. Reasonable doubt means a doubt based upon reason and common sense that arises from a fair and rational consideration of all the evidence or lack of evidence in the case. It is a doubt that is not a vague, speculative, or imaginary doubt, but such a doubt as would cause reasonable persons to hesitate to act in matters of importance to themselves.

8. The defendant is presumed to be innocent of the charges against him. This presumption remains with him throughout every stage of the trial and during your deliberations on the verdict. The presumption is not overcome until, from all the evidence in the case, you are convinced beyond a reasonable doubt that the defendant is guilty.

Additional Final Jury Instructions

9. The charge you must consider is the crime of Commercial Arson. In order to find the defendant guilty, you must find that the defendant, Arthur Jackson, either personally or through an agent, intentionally and willfully damaged by fire or explosion, a building or structure for the purpose of making a false insurance claim on behalf of Arthur Jackson or an entity controlled by, or owned by, Arthur Jackson. If you find that each of these elements has been proved beyond a reasonable doubt, then you shall find the defendant guilty of this charge. If you find that one or more of these elements have not been proved beyond a reasonable doubt, then you shall find the defendant not guilty of this charge.

   An agent is defined as a person who acts pursuant to the express direction of another person for the purpose of furthering the other person's specific intent.

10. (if applicable) The defendant has introduced evidence of his character and reputation for (truth and veracity) (being a peaceful and law-abiding citizen) (morality) (chastity) (honesty and integrity). This evidence may be sufficient, when considered with the other evidence in the case, to raise a reasonable doubt of the defendant's guilt. However, if from all the evidence in the case, you are satisfied beyond a reasonable doubt of the defendant's guilt, then it is your duty to find him guilty, even though he may have a good reputation for (truth and veracity) (being a peaceful and law-abiding citizen) (morality) (chastity) (honesty and integrity).

11. The Court did not in any way, and does not by these instructions, give or intimate any opinions as to what has or has not been proven in the case, or as to what are or are not the facts of the case.

No one of these instructions states all of the law applicable, but all of them must be taken, read, and considered together as they are connected with and related to each other as a whole.

You must not be concerned with the wisdom of any rule of law. Regardless of any opinions you may have as to what the law ought to be, it would be a violation of your sworn duty to base a verdict on any other view of the law than that given in the instructions of the court.

IN THE CIRCUIT COURT OF
DARROW COUNTY, STATE OF NITA
CRIMINAL DIVISION

THE STATE OF NITA,

v.   CASE NO. CR-70410-1

ARTHUR JACKSON,

Defendant.

COMMERCIAL ARSON

We, the jury, find the Defendant, Arthur Jackson, NOT GUILTY.

_____

Foreperson

We, the jury, find the Defendant, Arthur Jackson, GUILTY.

_____

Foreperson

Special Impeachment Problems

PROBLEM 1: MARIE WILLIAMS

Assume that Ms. Williams has testified at trial on direct examination that she was never bitter or angry at Mr. Jackson, and she just wanted the best for him when their relationship terminated.

(a) For the Defense, conduct a cross-examination and impeachment of Ms. Williams.

(b) For the State, conduct a redirect examination to the extent necessary to rehabilitate.

PROBLEM 2: MARIE WILLIAMS

Assume that Ms. Williams has testified at trial on direct examination that when she confronted Mr. Jackson with her suspicions that he had hired an arsonist, Mr. Jackson looked away from her and said, "Marie, you know the trouble I'm in." Assume further that Ms. Williams testified on direct that she went to the police "immediately" after this conversation with Mr. Jackson.

(a) For the Defense, conduct a cross-examination and impeachment of Ms. Williams.

(b) For the State, conduct a redirect examination to the extent necessary to rehabilitate.

PROBLEM 3: JOHN ANDERSON

Assume that Mr. Anderson has testified at trial on direct examination that when he asked Mr. Jackson for financial information on the company, Mr. Jackson said the information had already been compiled and would be brought to the bank the next day. Assume further that Mr. Anderson testified on direct that he asked Mr. Jackson for additional collateral for the loan, but Mr. Jackson said he had no additional collateral available, that he was "tapped out."

(a) For the Defense, conduct a cross-examination and impeachment of Mr. Anderson.

(b) For the State, conduct a redirect examination to the extent necessary to rehabilitate.

PROBLEM 4: ARTHUR JACKSON

Assume that Mr. Jackson has testified at trial on direct examination that he hired Mr. Avery based upon Ms. Peterson's recommendation and after he had called Yaphank and Fass to verify Mr. Avery's achievements.

(a) For the State, conduct a cross-examination and impeachment of Mr. Jackson.

(b) For the Defense, conduct a redirect examination to the extent necessary to rehabilitate.

PROBLEM 5: ARTHUR JACKSON

Assume that Mr. Jackson has testified at trial on direct examination that he never saw or spoke to George Avery on the night of the fire, and that he saw Marie Williams as he was leaving around 6:30 p.m.

(a) For the State, conduct a cross-examination and impeachment of Mr. Jackson.

(b) For the Defense, conduct a redirect examination to the extent necessary to rehabilitate.

PROBLEM 6: ARTHUR JACKSON

Assume that Mr. Jackson has testified at trial on direct examination that at the time of the fire he was already in the process of compiling the documents the bank wanted and that he had already contacted General Motors about the plans.

(a) For the State, conduct a cross-examination and impeachment of Mr. Jackson.

(b) For the Defense, conduct a redirect examination to the extent necessary to rehabilitate.

Special Exhibit Problems

The following exhibit problems are designed to be used on a stand-alone basis. They create or add facts or exhibits as necessary for use in a particular exhibit foundation. **They do not add or subtract any fact or issue from the main case file, and none of the exhibit problems are to be treated as changing the main case file in any way.**

Exhibit Problem 1

Assume that after the fire at Flinders was extinguished, and the firefighters had left the scene, Marie Williams went to the scene at 2:00 in the morning on November 17, YR-1. No one was with her. On May 20, YR-0, when Marie arrives at a joint state/defense agreed interview, she brings with her a partially melted and scorched plastic Prell shampoo bottle. There are liquid contents in the bottle, and the bottle is still intact. In black Sharpie, the initials "MW" and "11/17/YR-1–2:00 a.m." are written on the side of the bottle. Marie states that she found the shampoo bottle in the rubble on the side of the building where George Avery's office used to be. She states she opened the shampoo bottle, and it had a "funny acrid" smell that did not smell like Prell. She first put the bottle in her car for two weeks, and then she put it on a shelf in her garage until she brought it to her deposition. No one has a key to the garage except her handyman, her next-door-neighbor, and her best friend. After the deposition, the parties agree to a testing procedure for the contents of the bottle and for maintenance and preservation of the evidence, and stipulated to the accuracy of the lab's findings as to the chemical composition of the contents, but did not stipulate that the contents were present in the bottle as of November 17, YR-1. The jointly selected laboratory determined that the contents include Prell shampoo and an undetermined strong acid. Underneath the lid of the shampoo bottle, the laboratory determines that there is trace presence of hydrochloric acid.

For the State, offer the shampoo bottle and laboratory report into evidence.

For the Defense, oppose the offer.

Exhibit Problem 2

Assume that Flinders Aluminum required all of its employees and contractors, including George Avery, to undergo fire prevention and response training. The training included a demonstration on using buckets to extinguish fires. The buckets were kept in the HCl storage room shown on Exhibit 7, approximately twenty feet from the location where George Avery's body was found on November 16, YR-1, the night of the Flinders fire. On November 17, YR-1, after the fire scene had cooled, Fireman Henderson picked up the bucket shown next to the tape outline of George Avery's body in Exhibit 17. Henderson kept it in his evidence locker from that time until trial. He will testify that the bucket was empty when he picked it up. Arthur Jackson will testify that the bucket is one of the buckets kept in the HCl storage room, and used in fire response training for the employees that George Avery also attended.

A. For the Defense, lay a foundation and move the introduction of the bucket into evidence.

For the State, oppose the introduction of the bucket.

Assume that the bucket found at the scene and retrieved by Fireman Henderson has been lost.

For the Defense, lay a foundation and move the introduction of a bucket that is like the bucket shown in Exhibit 17.

For the State, oppose the introduction of the bucket.

Exhibit Problem 3

Exhibits 7, 8, 9, and 10 are the floor plan diagrams for the four floors of the Flinders plant. For the State, identify two issues/facts you would like to prove that involve the layout of the plant. Use one or more of the floor plans to assist in proving those two issues. Lay a foundation and offer the exhibit(s) and then, if admissibility is achieved, use the exhibit in some manner that helps your case. For the Defense, identify two issues/facts you would like to prove that involve the layout of the plant. Use one or more of the floor plans to assist in proving those two issues. Lay a foundation and offer the exhibit(s) and then, if admissibility is achieved, use the exhibit in some manner that helps your case. The Defense will oppose the proffer by the State, and vice versa. Develop all possible grounds for objection to the exhibit(s).

Exhibit Problem 4

Assume that Flinders maintained all invoice and payment records in its "cloud computing" account and that the bookkeeper would simply insert an electronic "Paid" date notation on all paid invoices. The State subpoenaed records from Flinders Aluminum seeking "true and accurate copies of all invoices for hydrochloric acid ordered by Flinders from 10/1/YR-2 to 11/30/YR-1." In response, Flinders produced the attached invoices from ChemGem, Inc., Nos. 10913 (Exhibit 1), 11009 (Exhibit 2), 11127 (Exhibit 3), 11323 (Exhibit 4), and 11450 (Exhibit 5). At trial, the State moves the admission of the invoices. The Defense objects.

A. For the State, establish the necessary foundation for admission of Exhibit 5, including if necessary the admission of the remaining exhibits.

B. For the Defense, make all available objections to preclude the admission of Exhibit 5 and any other offered invoices.

C. **Business records application:** For the Defense and the State: pick one of the invoices and establish a business records foundation for its admission into evidence; the opposing party will object to any deficiency in the business records foundation.

CHEMGEM, INC.

INVOICE 10913

To:

Newstart Fabrication Co.
187 River Road
Nita City, Nita   99997

Living better through chemistry

Product	Size	Price	Quantity	Shipped
Hydrochloric Acid	10 gal	$10.50	10	12/1/YR-2

TOTAL DUE: $105.00   **Payable in 30 days**

Pd. 12/10/YR-2 #1233

Thank you for your business!

1115 Industrial Plaza North
Nita City, Nita   99990
Visit our website: www.chemgem.nita

Telephone: 555-243-6436
(555-ChemGem)
Fax: 555-243-6435

Exhibit 1

CHEMGEM, INC.

INVOICE 11009

To:
Flinders Fabrication Co.
187 River Road
Nita City, Nita   99997

Living better through chemistry

Product	Size	Price	Quantity	Shipped
Hydrochloric Acid	10 gal	$10.50	10	3/1/YR-1

TOTAL DUE: **$105.00**   **Payable in 30 days**

Pd: 3/6/YR-1 # 1322

Thank you for your business!

1115 Industrial Plaza North
Nita City, Nita   99990
Visit our website: www.chemgem.nita

Telephone: 555-243-6436
(555-ChemGem)
Fax: 555-243-6435

Exhibit 2

CHEMGEM, INC.

INVOICE 11127

To:

Flinders Fabrication Co.
187 River Road
Nita City, Nita   99997

Living better through chemistry

Product	Size	Price	Quantity	Shipped
Hydrochloric Acid	10 gal	$10.50	10	6/1/YR-2

TOTAL DUE: $105.00   **Payable in 30 days**

Thank you for your business!

Pd. 6/9/YR-2 #1382

1115 Industrial Plaza North
Nita City, Nita   99990
Visit our website: www.chemgem.nita

Telephone: 555-243-6436
(555-ChemGem)
Fax: 555-243-6435

Exhibit
3

CHEMGEM, INC.

INVOICE 11323

To:
Flinders Fabrication Co.
187 River Road
Nita City, Nita   99997

Living better through chemistry

Product	Size	Price	Quantity	Shipped
Hydrochloric Acid	10 gal	$10.50	10	9/1/YR-2

TOTAL DUE: $105.00   **Payable in 30 days**

Thank you for your business!

 Pd. 9/16/YR-2 # 1423

1115 Industrial Plaza North   Telephone: 555-243-6436
Nita City, Nita   99990   (555-ChemGem)
Visit our website: www.chemgem.nita Fax: 555-243-6435

Exhibit

4

CHEMGEM, INC.

INVOICE 11450

To:

Newstart Fabrication Co.
187 River Road
Nita City, Nita   99997

Living better through chemistry

Product	Size	Price	Quantity	Shipped
Hydrochloric Acid	10 gal	$10.50	100	10/4/YR-2

TOTAL DUE: **$1050.00**   **Payable in 30 days**

Thank you for your business!

Pd. 10/14/YR-2 # 1479

1115 Industrial Plaza North
Nita City, Nita   99990
Visit our website: www.chemgem.nita

Telephone: 555-243-6436
(555-ChemGem)
Fax: 555-243-6435

Exhibit

5

Exhibit Problem 5

Assume that on December 13, YR-1, shortly after she was fired from Flinders, Marie Williams went to the Nita General Hospital emergency room with symptoms of a panic attack. She was treated by Dr. Jill Enderight, who is no longer working in Nita General and is no longer available. Attached as Exhibit 1 is the emergency room record. Marie Williams has now sued Flinders for wrongful termination including emotional distress and pain and suffering damages.

Representing Ms. Williams for purposes of this problem, move the admission of the medical record. Call the witness or witnesses you need to admit the medical record into evidence.

For Flinders, oppose the admission.

NITA GENERAL HOSPITAL

NITA CITY, NITA

Patient: Marie Williams   MRN: 11-0667754   Location of treatment: ED

Admitted: 12/13/YR-1   Date of Discharge: 12/13/YR-1   Rx Provided: Yes

Dictated: 12/13/YR-1   Transcribed: 12/14/YR-1   Ins.: BC/BS

PHYSICIAN PROGRESS NOTES

Patient admitted to emergency department at 1623 with complaints of heaviness and tightness in chest, "racing heart," and difficulty breathing. 12-lead EKG indicates sinus tachycardia at 110 bpm. No other abnormalities in rhythm and no indication of any current or impending cardiac event. Respirations slightly elevated at 22 per minute. Temperature within normal limits. O2 saturation 98% and normal. Blood pressure elevated at 144/98. Pt. is diaphoretic and skin is cool and pale. Pedal and radial pulses are normal and equal bilaterally.

Ms. Williams states her symptoms started during the night and worsened today, following her involuntary separation from her longtime employer, Flinders Fabrication. This pt. was last seen in ER in August YR-1 at which time she was diagnosed with a panic attack with symptoms similar to those on presentation today. At that time, pt. had been demoted, and her boss told her he was replacing her with "someone a lot more cooperative." Pt. was given therapeutic exercises to follow to assist her in responding to stressful events and was also given a prescription for Xanax p.o. Pt. indicates she has obtained general relief over the past several months although her workplace has been an extremely stressful environment and her symptoms have been exacerbated at times. Her company building burned down in November.

Pt. states that her boss has now recently fired her after she accused him and a co-worker of burning down the building on purpose. Pt. states that her boss admitted the arson, but then tried to deny it, which caused pt. to be fearful and anxious. Since her firing, pt.'s symptoms have been exacerbated. Pt. was given Rx for Valium and Ambien. Pt. referred to her regular provider for follow-up.

/s/ Jill Enderight, MD

Certified as a true and correct copy of the original in the files of Nita General Hospital. Pursuant to N.G.S. § 47-322(A) (YR-3 Repl. Pamp.), the original of all medical records must remain in the custody of the treating hospital.

Hilda Burns

Hilda Burns
Director and Custodian, Medical Records   EXHIBIT 1
Nita General Hospital

Thumbnails of PowerPoint Slides

Slide 1

REVISED CRIMINAL CODE

Section 672.7 Commercial Arson

1. A person commits the crime of commercial arson if the person personally or through an agent, intentionally and willfully damages by fire or explosion a building or structure for the purpose of making a false insurance claim that would benefit the person or an entity controlled by, or owned by, the person.

2. Commercial Arson is a felony punishable by confinement in prison for a minimum period of ten years and a maximum period of twenty-five years, a fine of up to $10,000, or both.

Section 842.4 Conspiracy to Commit a Felony

1. A person commits the crime of conspiracy to commit a felony if the person agrees with another person to act together to commit an offense that is punishable as a felony, and that either the person or the other commits an act that is pursuant to the plan to commit the felonious offense.

2. Conspiracy to commit a felony is a felony that is punishable by confinement in prison for a period up to ten years, or a fine of $5,000, or both.

Slide 2

Section 672.7 Commercial Arson

1. A person commits the crime of commercial arson if the person personally or through an agent, intentionally and willfully damages by fire or explosion a building or structure for the purpose of making a false insurance claim that would benefit the person or an entity controlled by, or owned by, the person.

2. Commercial Arson is a felony punishable by confinement in prison for a minimum period of ten years and a maximum period of twenty-five years, a fine of up to $10,000, or both.

Slide 3

Section 842.4 Conspiracy to Commit a Felony

1. A person commits the crime of conspiracy to commit a felony if the person agrees with another person to act together to commit an offense that is punishable as a felony, and that either the person or the other commits an act that is pursuant to the plan to commit the felonious offense.

2. Conspiracy to commit a felony is a felony that is punishable by confinement in prison for a period up to ten years, or a fine of $5,000, or both.

Slide 4

Slide 5

1. The defendant shall plead guilty to one (1) count of conspiracy as charged in the amended information filed in this cause. The Court shall adjudicate the defendant guilty and sentence the defendant to three years of probation. The defendant's plea of guilty shall be irrevocable.

Slide 6

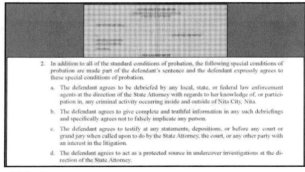

Slide 7

2. In addition to all of the standard conditions of probation, the following special conditions of probation are made part of the defendant's sentence and the defendant expressly agrees to these special conditions of probation.

   a. The defendant agrees to be debriefed by any local, state, or federal law enforcement agents at the direction of the State Attorney with regards to her knowledge of, or participation in, any criminal activity occurring inside and outside of Nita City, Nita.

   b. The defendant agrees to give complete and truthful information in any such debriefings and specifically agrees not to falsely implicate any person.

   c. The defendant agrees to testify at any statements, depositions, or before any court or grand jury when called upon to do by the State Attorney, the court, or any other party with an interest in the litigation.

   d. The defendant agrees to act as a protected source in undercover investigations at the direction of the State Attorney.

Slide 8

Slide 9

4. The parties agree that this agreement provides immunity from prosecution of the defendant for her direct or indirect involvement as a principal in the crime charged in the initial information.

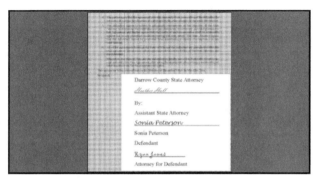

Slide 10

Darrow County State Attorney

Heather Hall

By:

Assistant State Attorney

Sonia Peterson

Sonia Peterson

Defendant

Ryan Jones

Attorney for Defendant

Slide 11

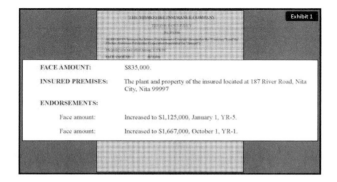

Slide 12

Exhibit 1

FACE AMOUNT:	$835,000.
INSURED PREMISES:	The plant and property of the insured located at 187 River Road, Nita City, Nita 99997
ENDORSEMENTS:	
Face amount:	Increased to $1,125,000, January 1, YR-5.
Face amount:	Increased to $1,667,000, October 1, YR-1.

Slide 13

Slide 14

Slide 15

Slide 16

Slide 17

Slide 18

Slide 19

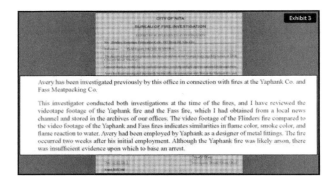

Avery has been investigated previously by this office in connection with fires at the Yaphank Co. and Fass Meatpacking Co.

This investigator conducted both investigations at the time of the fires, and I have reviewed the videotape footage of the Yaphank fire and the Fass fire, which I had obtained from a local news channel and stored in the archives of our offices. The video footage of the Flinders fire compared to the video footage of the Yaphank and Fass fires indicates similarities in flame color, smoke color, and flame reaction to water. Avery had been employed by Yaphank as a designer of metal fittings. The fire occurred two weeks after his initial employment. Although the Yaphank fire was likely arson, there was insufficient evidence upon which to base an arrest.

Slide 20

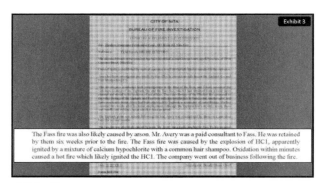

The Yaphank plant was rebuilt following the fire. Avery was re-employed by them on a part-time basis for several months.

Slide 21

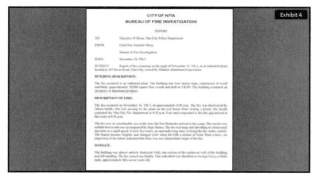

The Fass fire was also likely caused by arson. Mr. Avery was a paid consultant to Fass. He was retained by them six weeks prior to the fire. The Fass fire was caused by the explosion of HC1, apparently ignited by a mixture of calcium hypochlorite with a common hair shampoo. Oxidation within minutes caused a hot fire which likely ignited the HC1. The company went out of business following the fire.

Slide 22

This could have been the setup at Flinders. The traces of the igniter in this case were likely washed away by the fire hoses. However, it appears that one of the machines in the shop had been operating just prior to the fire. HC1 combining with hot metal can create an explosive situation.

Slide 23

Slide 24

Slide 25

Slide 26

Slide 27

Slide 28

Slide 29

Slide 30

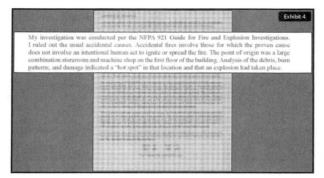

My investigation was conducted per the NFPA 921 Guide for Fire and Explosion Investigations. I ruled out the usual accidental causes. Accidental fires involve those for which the proven cause does not involve an intentional human act to ignite or spread the fire. The point of origin was a large combination storeroom and machine shop on the first floor of the building. Analysis of the debris, burn patterns, and damage indicated a "hot spot" in that location and that an explosion had taken place.

Slide 31

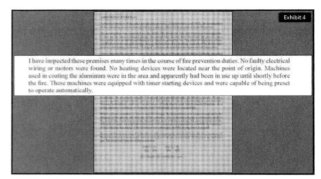

I have inspected these premises many times in the course of fire prevention duties. No faulty electrical wiring or motors were found. No heating devices were located near the point of origin. Machines used in coating the aluminum were in the area and apparently had been in use up until shortly before the fire. These machines were equipped with timer starting devices and were capable of being preset to operate automatically.

Slide 32

When a plastic container or liner is used for storage, the hydrochloric acid cannot compromise the integrity of the plastic and leak out of the container. This is because plastic is chemically inert to the acid. Glass could also be used, but problems arise with the tendency for glass to break and the difficulty of repair. An acid leak would occur if the container was ruptured (by a forklift, for instance), if the container was faulty, if the container was sabotaged, or if the wrong drum was used.

Slide 33

Serious problems may arise if hydrochloric acid is improperly stored and leaks out of its container. If the acid contacts a ferrous metal, such as steel, then hydrogen is generated. Hydrogen is an explosive gas. The chemical formula of this reaction is:

$$2HCl + Fe \qquad FeCl_2 + H_2$$
$$(L) \quad (S) \qquad (S) \quad (G)$$

(L) = liquid; (S) = solid; (G) = gas

Slide 34

Slide 35

The reddish brown color of the smoke, together with the large flames, indicates that substances containing nitrocellulose fiber, sulfur, or sulfuric, nitric, or hydrochloric acid were burning. The fact that flames burned brighter and changed color when hit with water is another indication that an accelerant was used. Difficulty in extinguishing the fire also points to the use of an accelerant. A chemical analysis of the ashes showed that hydrochloric acid, an explosive substance when combined with hot metal, in fact was burning. When HCl comes in contact with ferrous metals, hydrogen is released, and when hydrogen is combined with air, it may cause an explosive situation. Although hydrochloric acid is normally present in the plant, scarring of the concrete floor plus chemical analysis showed that an unusually large amount was located at the point of origin of the fire. Moreover, the magnitude of the fire and its rapid spreading indicate that several hundred gallons of the acid likely were splashed about the source of the fire. Normally, a plant of this type and size would maintain a supply of approximately fifty gallons of hydrochloric acid for cleaning purposes. This would likely be stored in one place. Analysis of the debris indicates an explosion at the point of origin, likely caused by a time release igniter, possibly the preset timer of one of the machines or calcium hypochlorite mixed with shampoo.

Slide 36

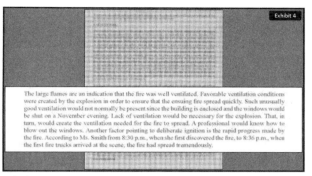

The large flames are an indication that the fire was well ventilated. Favorable ventilation conditions were created by the explosion in order to ensure that the ensuing fire spread quickly. Such unusually good ventilation would not normally be present since the building is enclosed and the windows would be shut on a November evening. Lack of ventilation would be necessary for the explosion. That, in turn, would create the ventilation needed for the fire to spread. A professional would know how to blow out the windows. Another factor pointing to deliberate ignition is the rapid progress made by the fire. According to Ms. Smith from 8:30 p.m., when she first discovered the fire, to 8:36 p.m., when the first fire trucks arrived at the scene, the fire had spread tremendously.

Slide 37

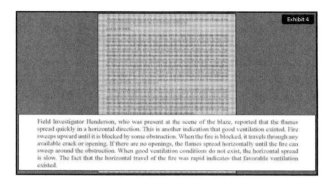

Field Investigator Henderson, who was present at the scene of the blaze, reported that the flames spread quickly in a horizontal direction. This is another indication that good ventilation existed. Fire sweeps upward until it is blocked by some obstruction. When the fire is blocked, it travels through any available crack or opening. If there are no openings, the flames spread horizontally until the fire can sweep around the obstruction. When good ventilation conditions do not exist, the horizontal spread is slow. The fact that the horizontal travel of the fire was rapid indicates that favorable ventilation existed.

Slide 38

Slide 39

Our investigation of Avery showed that he had been linked to two other fires that were of incendiary origin. One fire destroyed a factory owned by the Yaphank Co. Mr. Avery had been employed by Yaphank for only two weeks prior to the fire. The other fire destroyed a warehouse at the Fass Meatpacking Co. Although these fires were likely the result of arson, there was insufficient evidence for an arrest. Mr. Avery, who was associated with these businesses when the fires occurred, was questioned on both occasions. This marshal conducted both investigations. In connection with this investigation, I reviewed Avery's resumé which I obtained from John Anderson at First Trust Bank. I checked with Cornell and MIT, schools Avery indicated on his resumé he had graduated from. Neither had any record of George Avery.

Slide 40

Contrary to popular belief, a substantial number of arsonists are trapped and killed in their own fires. For the most part, these persons are less than skilled at the techniques of arson. It is less likely that a professional arsonist would be caught in his own fire, but not particularly unusual.

Slide 41

CONCLUSION:

This marshal concludes that the fire was the result of arson. This conclusion is based upon the following factors:

1. The unusually large amount of hydrochloric acid that was located at the point of origin of the fire and apparently splashed about the room. Hydrogen likely was released and, in combination with ferrous metal, exploded by some sort of time release device that malfunctioned.

2. The unusually rapid spread of the fire, caused by favorable ventilation conditions not normally present.

3. The presence of George Avery in the building at the time of the fire.

Submitted by:

Donald Olsen

Donald Olsen
Chief Fire Marshal

Slide 42

Slide 43

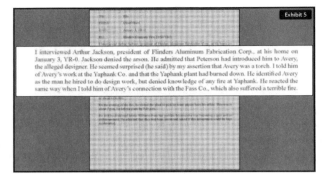

I interviewed Arthur Jackson, president of Flinders Aluminum Fabrication Corp., at his home on January 3, YR-0. Jackson denied the arson. He admitted that Peterson had introduced him to Avery, the alleged designer. He seemed surprised (he said) by my assertion that Avery was a torch. I told him of Avery's work at the Yaphank Co. and that the Yaphank plant had burned down. He identified Avery as the man he hired to do design work, but denied knowledge of any fire at Yaphank. He reacted the same way when I told him of Avery's connection with the Fass Co., which also suffered a terrible fire.

Slide 44

He admitted paying Avery $10,000.

He admitted that HCl was kept at the plant in quantities of about fifty gallons.

I asked him if he personally checked on Avery's credentials listed on his résumé or any references Avery may have supplied. He said he left such matters to Ms. Peterson.

He said he had no motive because his wife had assets of around $300,000 and he had personal assets of about $150,000.

Slide 45

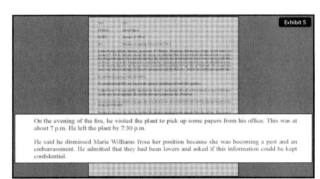

On the evening of the fire, he visited the plant to pick up some papers from his office. This was at about 7 p.m. He left the plant by 7:30 p.m.

He said he dismissed Marie Williams from her position because she was becoming a pest and an embarrassment. He admitted that they had been lovers and asked if this information could be kept confidential.

Slide 46

Slide 47

Slide 48

Slide 49

Slide 50

Slide 51

Slide 52

Slide 53

Slide 54

Slide 55

Slide 56

Slide 57

Slide 58

Slide 59

Slide 60

Slide 61

Slide 62

Slide 63

Slide 64

Slide 65

Slide 66

The upper extremities are remarkable in that there are first- and second-degree burns over the skin of the hands and distal forearms, and there is a compound fracture of the right humerus.

Slide 67

Slide 68

The torso is remarkable in that there are numerous fractures of the ribs bilaterally that can be palpated through the skin. There are three small ecchymoses over the left pectoral region and there are numerous superficial scrapes over the skin of the lumbar region. On the back there is a three-inch in diameter circular contusion that is definitely patterned and is essentially a series of 1 cm arcs that form a "broken circle." It is located over the right scapula.

Slide 69

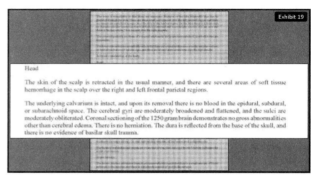

Head

The skin of the scalp is retracted in the usual manner, and there are several areas of soft tissue hemorrhage in the scalp over the right and left frontal parietal regions.

The underlying calvarium is intact, and upon its removal there is no blood in the epidural, subdural, or subarachnoid space. The cerebral gyri are moderately broadened and flattened, and the sulci are moderately obliterated. Coronal sectioning of the 1250 gram brain demonstrates no gross abnormalities other than cerebral edema. There is no herniation. The dura is reflected from the base of the skull, and there is no evidence of basilar skull trauma.

Slide 70

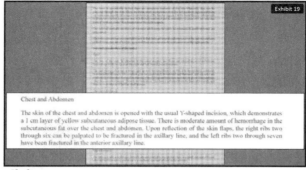

Chest and Abdomen

The skin of the chest and abdomen is opened with the usual Y-shaped incision, which demonstrates a 1 cm layer of yellow subcutaneous adipose tissue. There is moderate amount of hemorrhage in the subcutaneous fat over the chest and abdomen. Upon reflection of the skin flaps, the right ribs two through six can be palpated to be fractured in the axillary line, and the left ribs two through seven have been fractured in the anterior axillary line.

Slide 71

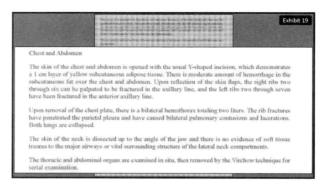

Chest and Abdomen

The skin of the chest and abdomen is opened with the usual Y-shaped incision, which demonstrates a 1 cm layer of yellow subcutaneous adipose tissue. There is moderate amount of hemorrhage in the subcutaneous fat over the chest and abdomen. Upon reflection of the skin flaps, the right ribs two through six can be palpated to be fractured in the axillary line, and the left ribs two through seven have been fractured in the anterior axillary line.

Upon removal of the chest plate, there is a bilateral hemothorax totaling two liters. The rib fractures have penetrated the parietal pleura and have caused bilateral pulmonary contusions and lacerations. Both lungs are collapsed.

The skin of the neck is dissected up to the angle of the jaw and there is no evidence of soft tissue trauma to the major airways or vital surrounding structure of the lateral neck compartments.

The thoracic and abdominal organs are examined in situ, then removed by the Virchow technique for serial examination.

Slide 72

Slide 73

Slide 74

Slide 75

Slide 76

Slide 77

Slide 78

Slide 79

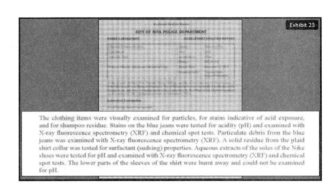

Slide 80

Laboratory Examination

The following items were received:

Item 1, a blue plaid shirt with burnt sleeves

Item 2, blue jeans

Item 3, white briefs

Item 4, white crew socks

Item 5, a pair of white Nike athletic shoes

Slide 81

The clothing items were visually examined for particles, for stains indicative of acid exposure, and for shampoo residue. Stains on the blue jeans were tested for acidity (pH) and examined with X-ray fluorescence spectrometry (XRF) and chemical spot tests. Particulate debris from the blue jeans was examined with X-ray fluorescence spectrometry (XRF). A solid residue from the plaid shirt collar was tested for surfactant (sudsing) properties. Aqueous extracts of the soles of the Nike shoes were tested for pH and examined with X-ray fluorescence spectrometry (XRF) and chemical spot tests. The lower parts of the sleeves of the shirt were burnt away and could not be examined for pH.

Slide 82

Slide 83

Examination Conclusions and Observations

No indications of hydrochloric acid, such as acidity or chloride, were found on the blue jeans or the soles of the Nike shoes. This does not mean the items were not exposed to hydrochloric acid under circumstances in which it did not survive on the clothing, such as dilution or exposure to heat. A variety of metallic particles were found on the blue jeans, including aluminum, iron, and some with a composition of iron, nickel, and chromium, which are found in stainless steel. The solid residue from the left shirt collar exhibited sudsing properties when mixed with water, as would be expected from shampoo or soap products. No other tests were performed on the solid residue. This laboratory cannot determine the brand of shampoo.

Slide 84

Slide 85

Slide 86

Slide 87

Slide 88

Slide 89

Slide 90

Slide 91

Slide 92

Slide 93

Slide 94

Slide 95

Slide 96

Slide 97

Slide 98

Exhibit 29

I have had several meetings this month with Arthur Jackson, President of Flinders Aluminum, in which he has requested new financing and an adjustment of current financing with the bank. I have reviewed the proposed concept of transitioning the Flinders Aluminum plant that currently manufactures siding for housing to an auto parts manufacturing plant and am seeking additional information from our client in this regard. Given the admitted recent earnings track record at Flinders, the time has come for such a transition and, if handled deftly, this could be a very promising investment. I have asked the client to provide financial data, market studies, tax returns, and product designs (surprisingly, none have been provided to date), which, if they pan out, will encourage our participation. The land value alone in this riverfront area could provide the requisite security for any investment.

Slide 99

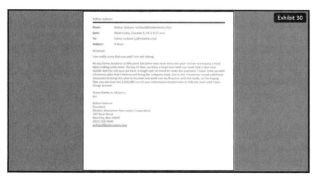

Slide 100

Exhibit 30

As you know, business at the plant has been very slow since last year and we are having a hard time making ends meet. On top of that, we have a large loan with our bank that is due next month and I'm not sure we have enough cash on hand to make the payment. I have come up with a business plan that I believe will bring the company back, but in the meantime I need additional resources to bring this plan to fruition and work out my finances with the bank, so I'm hoping that you can loan me $100,000 out of your inheritance investments to tide me over until I turn things around.

Slide 101

Slide 102

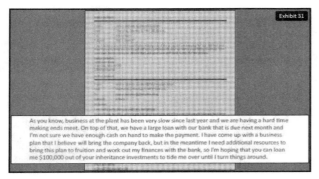

As you know, business at the plant has been very slow since last year and we are having a hard time making ends meet. On top of that, we have a large loan with our bank that is due next month and I'm not sure we have enough cash on hand to make the payment. I have come up with a business plan that I believe will bring the company back, but in the meantime I need additional resources to bring this plan to fruition and work out my finances with the bank, so I'm hoping that you can loan me $100,000 out of your inheritance investments to tide me over until I turn things around.

Slide 103

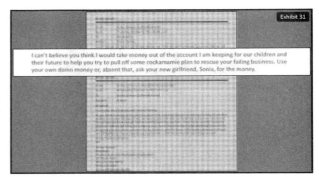

I can't believe you think I would take money out of the account I am keeping for our children and their future to help you try to pull off some cockamamie plan to rescue your failing business. Use your own damn money or, absent that, ask your new girlfriend, Sonia, for the money.

Slide 104

Slide 105

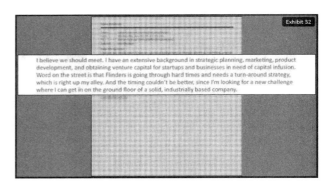

I believe we should meet. I have an extensive background in strategic planning, marketing, product development, and obtaining venture capital for startups and businesses in need of capital infusion. Word on the street is that Flinders is going through hard times and needs a turn-around strategy, which is right up my alley. And the timing couldn't be better, since I'm looking for a new challenge where I can get in on the ground floor of a solid, industrially based company.

Slide 106

Slide 107

Career Profile

Experienced Administrative Assistant with excellent organizational skills and emphasis on developing new businesses and product lines.

Slide 108

Slide 109

Slide 110

Slide 111

Slide 112

Slide 113

Slide 114

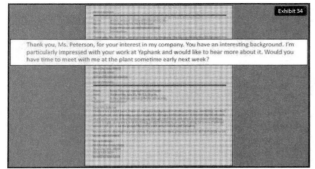

Thank you, Ms. Peterson, for your interest in my company. You have an interesting background. I'm particularly impressed with your work at Yaphank and would like to hear more about it. Would you have time to meet with me at the plant sometime early next week?

Slide 115

Slide 116

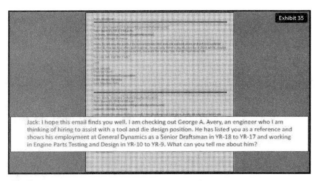

Jack: I hope this email finds you well. I am checking out George A. Avery, an engineer who I am thinking of hiring to assist with a tool and die design position. He has listed you as a reference and shows his employment at General Dynamics as a Senior Draftsman in YR-18 to YR-17 and working in Engine Parts Testing and Design in YR-10 to YR-9. What can you tell me about him?

Slide 117

Matt: To tell you the truth, I do not remember him well. He worked alone and did not socialize either during work or after with anyone. He was only there in my division for a short while, maybe three or four months before he left. His work for us was fine. I wish I had more info.

Slide 118

Slide 119

Slide 120

Slide 121

Slide 122

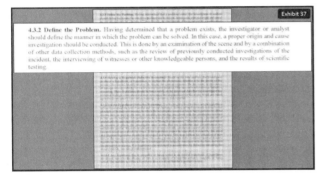

4.3.2 Define the Problem. Having determined that a problem exists, the investigator or analyst should define the manner in which the problem can be solved. In this case, a proper origin and cause investigation should be conducted. This is done by an examination of the scene and by a combination of other data collection methods, such as the review of previously conducted investigations of the incident, the interviewing of witnesses or other knowledgeable persons, and the results of scientific testing.

Slide 123

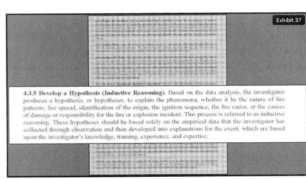

4.3.5 Develop a Hypothesis (Inductive Reasoning). Based on the data analysis, the investigator produces a hypothesis, or hypotheses, to explain the phenomena, whether it be the nature of fire patterns, fire spread, identification of the origin, the ignition sequence, the fire cause, or the causes of damage or responsibility for the fire or explosion incident. This process is referred to as inductive reasoning. These hypotheses should be based solely on the empirical data that the investigator has collected through observation and then developed into explanations for the event, which are based upon the investigator's knowledge, training, experience, and expertise.

Slide 124

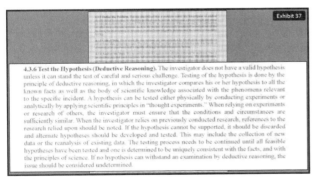

4.3.6 Test the Hypothesis (Deductive Reasoning). The investigator does not have a valid hypothesis unless it can stand the test of careful and serious challenge. Testing of the hypothesis is done by the principle of deductive reasoning, in which the investigator compares his or her hypothesis to all the known facts as well as the body of scientific knowledge associated with the phenomena relevant to the specific incident. A hypothesis can be tested either physically by conducting experiments or analytically by applying scientific principles in "thought experiments." When relying on experiments or research of others, the investigator must ensure that the conditions and circumstances are sufficiently similar. When the investigator relies on previously conducted research, references to the research relied upon should be noted. If the hypothesis cannot be supported, it should be discarded and alternate hypotheses should be developed and tested. This may include the collection of new data or the reanalysis of existing data. The testing process needs to be continued until all feasible hypotheses have been tested and one is determined to be uniquely consistent with the facts, and with the principles of science. If no hypothesis can withstand an examination by deductive reasoning, the issue should be considered undetermined.

Slide 125

Slide 126

Slide 127

Slide 128

Slide 129

Slide 130

Slide 131

Slide 132

Slide 133

Slide 134

Slide 135

Slide 136

Slide 137

Slide 138

Slide 139

Slide 140

Slide 141

Slide 142

Slide 143

Slide 144

Slide 145

Slide 146

Slide 147

Slide 148

Slide 149

Slide 150

Slide 151

Slide 152

Slide 153

Slide 154

Slide 155

Slide 156

Slide 157

Slide 158

Slide 159

Slide 160

Slide 161

Slide 162

Slide 163

Slide 164

Slide 165

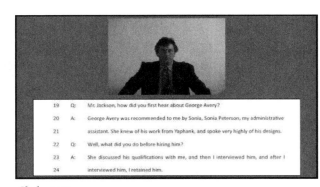

Slide 166

Slide 167

Slide 168

Slide 169

Slide 170

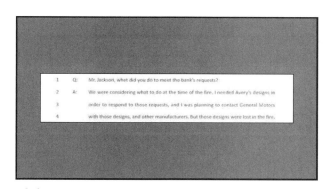

10	Q:	Who did you talk to before you left that night?
11	A:	I talked with George Avery. It was about 6:45 p.m.
12	Q:	What did he say to you?
13	A:	He said that he was going to work a little longer.
14	Q:	Did you say anything back to him?
15	A:	No, I didn't. That was normal.
16	Q:	Did you see anybody else before you left that night?
17	A:	As a matter of fact, I did. I bumped into Marie Williams.
18	Q:	What time was that?
19	A:	That was closer to 7 o'clock.
20	Q:	What did you say to her?
21	A:	Well, she doesn't usually work late, and actually I thought she looked really tired. And
22		I said, "Marie, you look beat. You ought to go home."

Slide 171

1	Q:	Mr. Jackson, what did you do to meet the bank's requests?
2	A:	We were considering what to do at the time of the fire. I needed Avery's designs in
3		order to respond to those requests, and I was planning to contact General Motors
4		with those designs, and other manufacturers. But those designs were lost in the fire.

Slide 172

Slide 173

Slide 174

Slide 175

Slide 176

Slide 177

Slide 178

Slide 179

Exhibit Slides
for
Special Exhibit Problems

Slide 180

Slide 181

Slide 182

Slide 183

Slide 184

Slide 185

Slide 186

Argument Slides

Slide 187

The State has the
burden of proving the guilt of
the defendant
beyond a reasonable doubt.

Slide 188

The defendant is not required
to prove his innocence.

Slide 189

David Pinkus - Expert Witness

"In arson investigation, no
finding of arson can be made
until _all_ possible accidental
causes are ruled out."

Slide 190

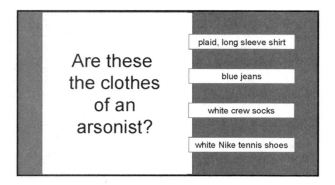

Are these
the clothes
of an
arsonist?

plaid, long sleeve shirt

blue jeans

white crew socks

white Nike tennis shoes

Slide 191

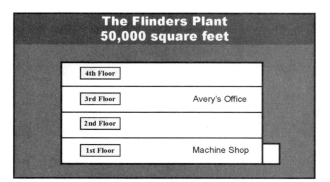

**The Flinders Plant
50,000 square feet**

4th Floor	
3rd Floor	Avery's Office
2nd Floor	
1st Floor	Machine Shop

Slide 192

Slide 193

Slide 194

Slide 195

Slide 196

Slide 197

Slide 198

Slide 199

The Collapse of Flinders Aluminum

YR-4 to YR-2	*Aluminum siding market collapses*
YR-2	*Flinders loses $500,000*
YR-1	*Flinders loses another $500,000 in first 9 months*
July YR-1	*Arthur Jackson: "…we're going under"*
July-Nov YR-1	*Jackson complains of financial problems*
Sept YR-1	*Jackson hires Avery*
Sept YR-1	*Jackson ups fire insurance coverage*
Oct YR-1	*Bank says "NO"*
Nov 16, YR-1	*FIRE destroys the plant*
Nov 28, YR-1	*$400,000 loan due*

Slide 200

Avery's Job History

Fass Meatpacking

6 Weeks

Yaphank

2 Weeks

Flinders

6 Weeks

Slide 201

"Arson" -- *Initial Reasons*

✓ Unusually large amount of hydrochloric acid
✓ Unusually rapid spread of the fire
✓ Presence of George Avery

Slide 202

"Arson" -- *Final Reasons*

✓ Unusually large amount of hydrochloric acid
✓ Unusually rapid spread of the fire
✓ Presence of George Avery
✓ Financial condition of the company
✓ Timing of increase in insurance
✓ Due date for $400,000 loan
✓ Avery is a stranger – No background check
✓ Bank says "No" – No plans, financials, studies
✓ Jackson lies about available funds

Slide 203

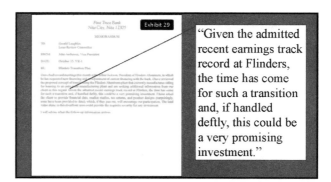

"Given the admitted recent earnings track record at Flinders, the time has come for such a transition and, if handled deftly, this could be a very promising investment."

Slide 204

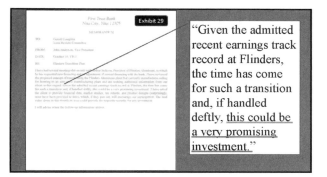

"Given the admitted recent earnings track record at Flinders, the time has come for such a transition and, if handled deftly, <u>this could be a very promising investment.</u>"

Slide 205

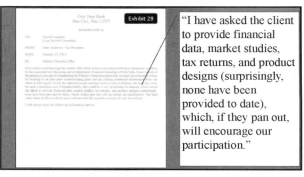

"I have asked the client to provide financial data, market studies, tax returns, and product designs (surprisingly, none have been provided to date), which, if they pan out, will encourage our participation."

Slide 206

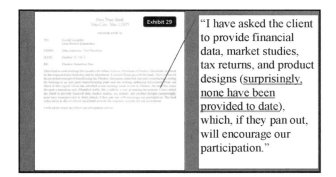

"I have asked the client to provide financial data, market studies, tax returns, and product designs (<u>surprisingly, none have been provided to date</u>), which, if they pan out, will encourage our participation."

Slide 207

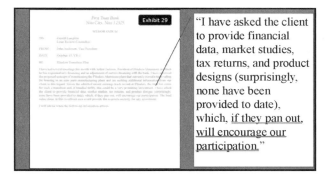

"I have asked the client to provide financial data, market studies, tax returns, and product designs (surprisingly, none have been provided to date), which, <u>if they pan out, will encourage our participation.</u>"

Slide 208

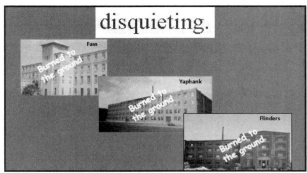

"The land value alone in this river front area could provide the requisite security for any investment."

Slide 209

Slide 210

Donald Olsen

- YR-25 to YR-20   Fireman, East Meadow Fire Department
  - Arson investigator for 2 years
- YR-20 to YR-10   Marshal, Arson bureau, East Meadow
- YR-10 to YR-5   Chief, Arson bureau, East Meadow
- YR-5-Present   Chief, Nita Fire Department
                    Bureau of Fire Investigation
- Investigated Flinders fire
- Subpoenaed to testify

Slide 211

David Pinkus

- YR-33 to YR-29   U S Navy, Fire fighting
  - Rank of Lieutenant
- YR-28 to YR-10   Firefighter & Investigator, Nita Fire Dept.
- YR-10 to YR-5   Deputy Fire Marshall, Nita City Bureau
  - In charge of Arson Investigation
- YR-5- Present   Forensic consultant, Lecturer
- Past President, Nita Association of Fire Fighters
- Publications on Arson Investigation

Slide 212

Chief Olsen	Mr. Pinkus
Chief, Nita Fire Dept.	Deputy under Olsen
Chief, Arson Bureau	Firefighter & investigator
East Meadow	Nita Fire Department
Investigated Flinders	Didn't
Talked with witnesses	Didn't
Talked with firefighters	Didn't
Sifted through rubble	Didn't
Experienced with Avery	Avery "disquieting"
Subpoenaed, not hired	Paid expert
Conclusion: Arson	"technically" not arson

Slide 213

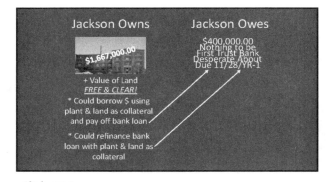

Slide 214